Thomas Cade Wadner

1885 - 1971

Captain, King's Royal Rifle Corps

Philip Wadner

2019

Published by Cade Books

©2019 Philip Wadner

All rights reserved.

ISBN 978-0-9931987-6-2

Philip Wadner has asserted his right under the Copyright, Designs and Patents Act 1988 to be identified as the author of this work.

This book is sold subject to the condition that it shall not, by way of trade or otherwise, be lent, resold, hired out, or otherwise circulated without the publisher's prior consent in any form of binding or cover other than that in which it is published and without a similar condition, including this condition, being imposed on the subsequent purchaser.

Front cover background: British Infantry awaiting advance to Mons. Photo: Unknown.

Front cover inset: Thomas Cade Wadner in KRRC uniform. Photo: Courtesy of Carol Cannell.

For my cousins.

Acknowledgements

This account would not have been possible without the extensive material available on the internet, and I express my gratitude to all those anonymous contributors who have made family history research possible in ways it has never been before.

I am especially indebted to the following people who helped with my research and the content of this book:

My cousins Sandra Edgeley, Carol Cannell, Jean Jackson, Michael Rushforth, Ian Rushforth and Peter Frossell for searching high and low for old family photographs and finding some gems. Hilary and Nigel Worker for exploring the churches and churchyards around Ravensden, the Staughtons and Grafham and for taking photographs. The staff at Bedfordshire Archives and Records Service, and the archivist at St. Mary's Church, Goldington, for answering queries and suggesting lines of enquiry. Paul Smith, landlord at The Polhill Arms, Renhold, for information about the interior of the pub and permission to use his photographs. Mike Collins, Patrick Linford and Parker Giggle (posthumously, because he was killed in action at the 3rd Battle of Ypres in WW1), for helping me to locate Council Cottages in Everton. Simon Hollands of Hollands Smith Estate Agents, Bedford for permission to use the photographs of 4 Dudley Street, Bedford. Colin Brett and Stephen Ellerbeck for the photograph of Glebe Farm before it was submerged under Grafham Water. Mike Edwards for his photograph of the Everton War Memorial. Jacqui Sullivan for the photograph of Sarah Green's gravestone. Bob Jewell for the old photograph of The Highway, Great Staughton. Pamela Hoole for discovering what happened to Great Uncle Arthur in Canada. Bob Webber for the photographs of Frederick Wadner and his family. John Wainwright for the photograph of Goldington Green School. Colin Woolf, a 'friend of Foster Hill Road Cemetery'. And finally my wife Christine, and friend and author Dr. John Craddock, for their encouragement and for reading and commenting on my drafts.

Preface

Like so many people who are driven to discover the past of a family member, I left it far too late. It is with deep regret that I missed the opportunity to discover more about my grandfather's life before he died in 1971. The loss of his father at the age of ten, and the break-up of the family home when he was sixteen after his mother re-married must have been difficult. His capture at the 1st Battle of Ypres in November 1914 would have been a dreadful experience, and to spend four years in POW camps nothing less than appalling. I am sorry I never asked, because until recently I didn't even know any of these things had happened.

It is almost impossible these days to be alive without leaving an electronic trail, and no-one needs a sniffer dog or a qualification in off-grid survival to follow it. Computers, the internet, and digitised records make it virtually impossible to hide from a persistent tracker. What is more amazing, though, is that the same technology can find trails left many years before the digital revolution and well before the internet existed. It needs more patience, more intuition and more luck, but the trails can often be uncovered.

The pages that follow include material which I know to be true, but occasionally include matter which I have elaborated upon, conjured up over the years in my own mind, or used some literary license because it felt right to do so. That does not mean this is a work of fiction. Like a portrait, it represents the facts through the eyes of the author.

When I began this book, I addressed my grandfather as Thomas. Even though there isn't a single occurrence of him using any other form of address in any of the records I have discovered, it sounded wrong. I had never heard him called Thomas, so I returned to the beginning and changed his name to Tom. I think it fits what I remember of his character far better. I hope he doesn't mind.

Contents

Introduction 1

Immediate Ancestry 5

    Mary Wadner - Tom's Paternal Grandmother 5

    John Cade - Tom's Maternal Grandfather 12

    Alice Wise - Tom's Maternal Grandmother 13

    Arthur Wadner - Tom's Father 15

    Amelia Cade - Tom's Mother 17

    Arthur and Amelia - Tom's Parents 18

    Goldington Highfields 21

    Death of Tom's Father - Jackman's Farm Tragedy 22

    Amelia and Jimmy Jones 28

The Early Years 35

    School 35

    Glebe Farm 40

    The Rose Inn 43

Army Service 47

    First World War 55

    Prisoner of War 65

    Repatriation 71

    War Medals 75

    Ceremonial Sword 77

Tom's Siblings 79

Rosa Ellen 80

Jim 83

Arthur 87

Frederick 91

The Middle Years 101

Violet Winifred Attersall - Tom's Wife 101

Marriage 105

Chapel Yard, Ravensden 108

Gladstone Street, Bedford 110

Marston Moretaine 112

The Polhill Arms 113

Everton 122

The Later Years 131

Dudley Street 131

Laxton's Nursery 134

The Castle Press 135

Retirement 138

Lovell Memorial Cottages 139

Descendants 145

References 152

SAMUEL SMITH		MARY WADNER
1837–1906	---MARRIED 1860---	1827–1881
LITTLE STAUGHTON		KIMBOLTON

ROSA ELLEN ODELL	JIM WADNER
1876–1929	1878–1937
NEWPORT PAGNELL	BEDFORD

WALTER J ODELL	LILY WADNER
1901–1942	1902–1976
MANCHESTER	BEDFORD

ARTHUR T ODELL	MAY WADNER
1902–1992	1906–1996
MILTON KEYNES	BEDFORD

ROSA ELLEN CROSS	ARTHUR J WADNER
1904–1987	1908–1930
NEW BRADWELL	BEDFORD

FREDERICK G ODELL	WILLIAM WADNER
1906–1980	1912–1999
NORTHAMPTON	BEDFORD

THOMAS G ODELL
1908–1997
DEVON

EMMA SHACKLEFORD
1909–1937
NORTHAMPTON

ENOS ODELL
1913–1990
NORTHAMPTON

FRANCIS ODELL
1913–2001
MILTON KEYNES

AMELIA CROOKES
1917–2007
SCUNTHORPE

FLORENCE LINDON
1919–2003
STONY STRATFORD

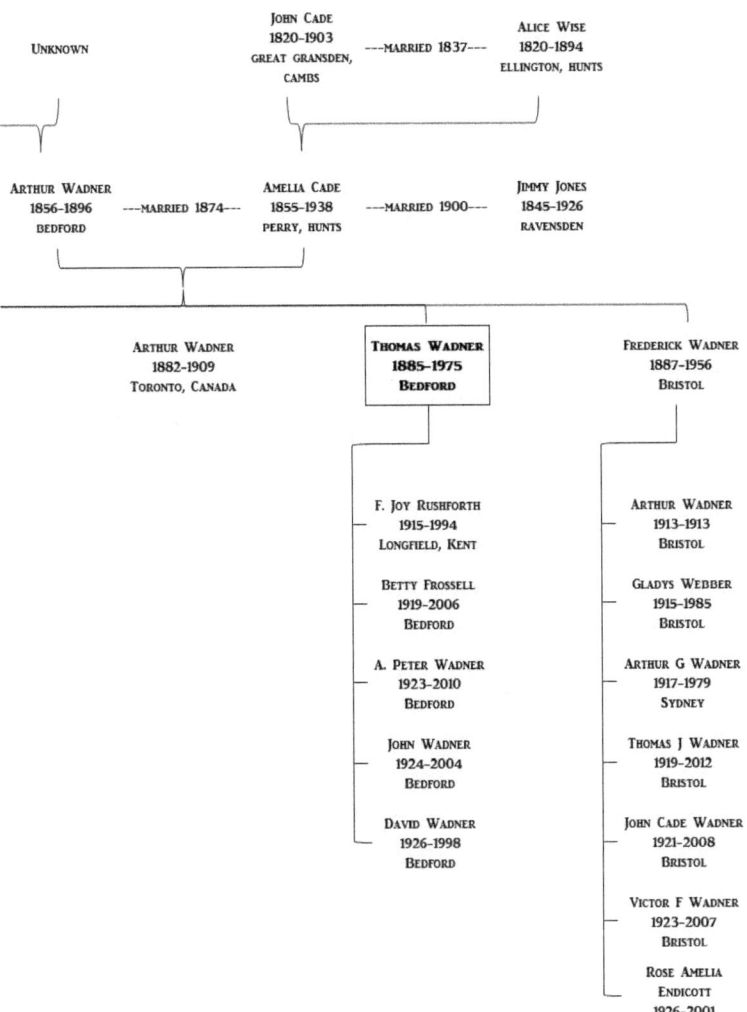

Introduction

James Wadner (1798-1847) was my great great great grandfather, and he worked as an agricultural labourer. So did his sons, their sons and their sons. My grandfather Thomas Cade Wadner (who I shall call Tom from this point on) left school at thirteen, and what did he do? He worked as an agricultural labourer.

We shouldn't be surprised. Agriculture was the largest male occupation in England during the nineteenth century[1]. Although many farms relied on day labourers employed on a casual basis, in rural Bedfordshire there was enough year-round work to employ a number of permanent workers and often these specific posts, such as horse keeper, shepherd, or cow man, came with the benefit of a cottage for the labourer and his family.

Agricultural labourers may not have been the most advantaged members of society, but their skills helped to build Bedfordshire into a flourishing rural county, albeit through the growth in wealth of landowners and to a lesser extent the farmers who owned or rented their holdings.

It was not only my grandfather's paternal ancestors who worked on the land. His maternal grandfather, John Cade (1820-1903), lived in Great Staughton and together with his two sons Joseph and John they were all agricultural labourers. His great grandfather, Wright Cade (1747-1825), great great grandfather Wright Cade (1709-1760), and back three more generations to his great great great great great grandfather William Wright (1650-1720) who lived in rural south Huntingdonshire, would all unquestionably have made their living working on a farm. William's wages would have been about two old pennies, or half a groat, for each day he worked. It was normal practice for the landowner to also supply a daily allowance of three or four pints of ale[2]. Tuppence earned in 1670 would be equivalent to about £16.50[3] today, far below the current minimum wage.

A quirk of fate made my research much easier than it would otherwise have been. My great grandfather Arthur Wadner was born outside marriage in 1856. His mother Mary Wadner married one Samuel Smith some four years later in 1860 and gave her son Samuel's surname. Arthur decided when he was older that, instead of Smith, he would return to using his mother's maiden name. Had it not been for that decision, instead of researching one of the most unusual surnames, I might have been looking for a needle trail amongst one of the most common names in the country's haystacks.

There are about 4.3 million Smiths in the world, 400,000 of them in England[4]. But there are only a few hundred Wadners, and most of them are in Brazil and Sweden[5]. The Ancestry website contains about 1000 birth, marriage and death records for Wadner, 1200 census records, and suggests there are some 542 member family trees containing the name[6].

Genealogists often warn that researching records can throw up some name variations, and looking for Wadners proved that true. Census records are particularly prone to variations, and in the 1881 return for Bolnhurst, Tom's father Arthur and his family are recorded as Wadnoe. Searching further back, in the 1841 return for Kimbolton, his great grandparents Jas (James) and Sarah and their family are written as Wadnor.

There is a very plausible reason for these variations. In the 1911 census, the head of the household became responsible for filling in the census form and therefore usually able to include an accurate surname. Before that, though, census enumerators visited each dwelling and filled out the census form on behalf of the householder.

Like most areas of England, Bedfordshire had its own dialect. Today, with the varied demographics of the area, the accent is no longer local. But in the 1800s, at its northern border with Huntingdonshire, the accent would have been a mix of East Midlands and Norfolk stirred in with an overflow of dialect from mid-Bedfordshire[7].

So, imagine an enumerator, possibly tired, cold or wet through, standing at the doorway of a cottage early in April. He (early censuses have 'Name of Enumerator, Mr......' pre-printed, so a female enumerator must have been a rarity) might even have been met with some suspicion as to the motive for wanting to know who was present in the house the previous night. He scribbles the names in a notebook as best he can make out from subdued strongly-accented mumbling. Then he returns home to transcribe the notes, probably pencilled and maybe smudged by bad weather, on to a census form.

Little wonder, then, that sometimes names were recorded incorrectly. The confusion doesn't end with censuses. Birth, marriage and death certificates were often originated by family members unable to sign the document. They would instead leave a mark, and trust that their name was not misheard by the registrar.

Genealogy is a time sponge. It can take countless hours poring over records to discover family links. My family tree contains around 500 people, with some going back to the mid-1600s. Exploring relationships is addictive, and I was tempted to include more branches of the family in this book. However, this is not the place for them. It is for my grandfather along with his closest relatives.

I hope to have captured the feel and spirit of my grandfather's life, painted some images of times gone by, and triggered a few memories for the reader. Not only for those who have the honour of him being part of their ancestry, but for anyone whose life spanned uncertainty and challenge intersected by two world wars.

Phil Wadner
February 2019

Immediate Ancestry

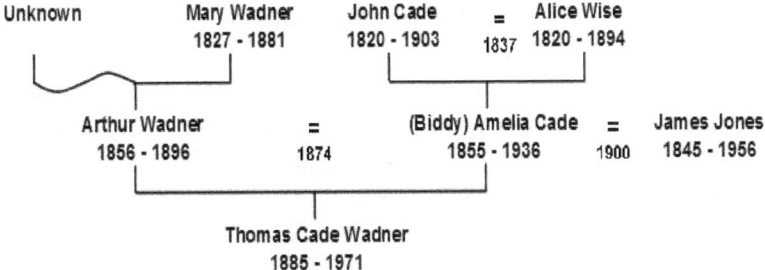

These are the people with whom the first part of this memoir is mostly associated. Tom's parents Arthur and Amelia, his grandmother Mary Wadner, and grandparents Alice Wise and John Cade who gave him his middle name. Mentioned later are Tom's brothers Frederick, Arthur and James and his sister Rosa. They played a significant part in his life as did Jimmy Jones, who Tom's mother married in 1900 four years after the death in tragic circumstances of his father.

Mary Wadner - Tom's Paternal Grandmother

Tom's paternal grandmother Mary Wadner was the first of nine children. She was born in 1827 to James Wadner, an agricultural labourer from Kimbolton, and his wife Sarah (née Martin). James and Sarah were married at St. Andrew's Church, Kimbolton on the 7th November 1825. Sarah's father William Martin was also an agricultural labourer, from Haddon, Huntingdonshire.

In 1841 at the age of fourteen, Mary was living with her parents James and Sarah, and her brothers and sisters William (13), Martha (9), George (6), Susan and Eliza (both 4), James (2) and Elisa (11 months) in Wornditch, a small hamlet with sixty five residents about a mile northwest of Kimbolton. Her sister Jane was to be born later that year, and Emily in 1843. Elisa died in 1848, aged eleven.

Kimbolton, straddling the River Kym, was a sleepy town in the nineteenth century, dependent almost entirely upon agriculture and lace making. There were three chapels for different religions and a grand thirteenth century church dedicated to St. Andrew at one end of the village. At the other end still stands Kimbolton Castle, in recent history the home of the Duke of Manchester. The castle is renowned as the place to which Catherine of Aragon was banished in April 1534 by Henry VIII for refusing to deny the legitimacy of her marriage, and she died there in January 1536.

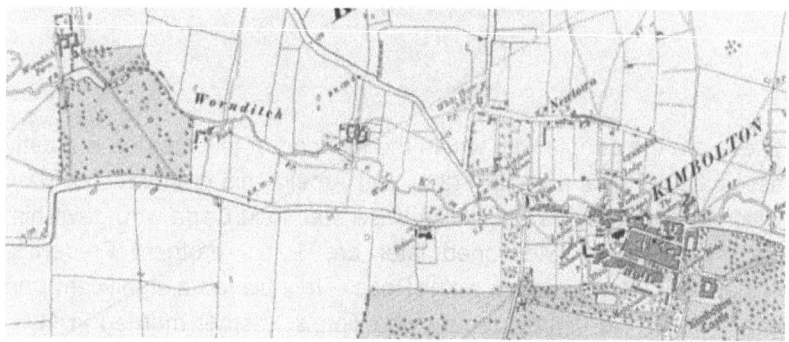

Kimbolton and Wornditch 1888. Map: National Library of Scotland

Most of the men in Wornditch will have worked as labourers at one of the nearby farms, either Wornditch Farm or Vicarage Farm to the north. This was not entirely the case though, because there was also a miller, shepherd, solicitor, and a relief officer probably charged with overseeing applications from the poor in nearby Kimbolton, as well as some residents of independent means.

Mary's father James died in August 1847 at the age of forty nine. Money will have been short, and her mother Sarah moved the family to a smaller cottage in Newtown on the northern edge of Kimbolton, making a living as a charwoman. Mary left home in 1851 at twenty four years old, to become a house servant to John Costin (47) and his wife Susan (46), daughter Elizabeth Ellen (21) and son John (10). John Costin was a General Clerk living on Kimbolton High Street.

Mary's sister Martha was also in service, with Benjamin and Sarah Bull who lived in Back Street, Kimbolton. Benjamin Bull was a farmer of moderate means, holding 18 acres of land. Sister Susan stayed at home and at the age of fourteen helped supplement the family's income as a lace maker. As soon as she was old enough, Susan also went into service. Her first position was at Wollaston, a couple of miles south of Wellingborough, where she was a cook to William Harris, a farmer of 168 acres. Ten years later she moved to Eastbourne as a cook and domestic servant to three sisters, Harriet, Eliza and Sarah Norris, all of independent means.

Mary became pregnant with Tom's father in 1855. She was unmarried, and if she had still been working as a servant for the Costins would probably have been instantly dismissed to avoid any finger pointing. However, the son was only ten years old and the head of the household would surely not have risked the scandal which would have resulted had he been involved. In any case, as Kimbolton was her home town, Mary would almost certainly have had relationships outside of her work.

In the 1840s about a third of women were pregnant at the time of their marriage and around one in twelve bore an illegitimate child [8]. Until a change in the law in 1875, it was illegal on moral and religious grounds to publish or distribute birth control literature, and punishments were severe. The availability of such information would not have helped Mary though, because she was illiterate. Anyway, birth control methods which are widely available today were not accessible when Mary was a young woman.

If the father of an illegitimate child was known, it was customary to apply considerable pressure to hasten a marriage to relieve any burden on the woman's parents. If the child's father was unknown, and the parents were unable to provide financial support, as would have been the case with Mary's mother, the parish would step in. Using taxpayer's money in this way was not a popular course of action, and if at all possible the father would be sought out and a knobstick wedding would be arranged, its name taken from the staff of office carried by the church warden charged with ensuring a marriage took place[9]. That was clearly not an option with Mary, because either she did not know the identity of the father, or was not telling.

Any attempt to identify who was responsible for Mary's pregnancy would be pure conjecture. Servants in the mid nineteenth century were often mistreated and vulnerable to being sexually exploited, not only by the members of the household where they worked, but also by their friends and visitors to their house. That is one possibility, but there are many others. It might be significant that Mary would not or could not say who the father was. Perhaps she had been threatened or bribed to keep the name of the father secret, or maybe she had been a victim of rape. Had the pregnancy been the result of a stable relationship, or even a casual association, she would probably have shared the name to secure financial help for the child's upbringing. Whatever the reason, nobody will ever be able to follow that line of the Wadner family ancestry.

Mary gave birth to a healthy son on the 21st August, 1856. She named him Arthur and registered his birth certificate using her own surname. Since Mary would have been paid a meagre wage as a servant, she would have been too poor to rent her own place. As a consequence, Arthur's first few years were probably spent in Mary's family home in Newtown, Kimbolton where her mother could help cope with the newborn and his initial upbringing.

Mary was illiterate, and where she would have signed Arthur's birth certificate there is a cross, with a note that it is her mark. The registrar would have asked Mary her name and written it for her. It seems he misheard her and it is given on the certificate as Mary Wadnoe.

Kimbolton will have attracted many neighbouring farmers, labourers and lace makers. Fairs were held four times each year, with a weekly market each Friday. It was probably at one of those fairs or market days that Mary first set eyes upon Samuel Smith of Little Staughton. Although Little Staughton stands less than four miles south east of Kimbolton, Mary would have had no particular reason to travel there.

Samuel Smith was born in 1837 so was ten years younger than Mary, but there must have been a significant spark between them because not only did they marry, but the bond lasted for the whole of their lives. Happily, after he reached the age of four, Arthur was to have a father as he grew up.

Mary and Samuel's wedding took place on Friday the 16th November 1860 at St. Margaret's, Little Staughton Parish Church. The church is thirteenth century, and although originally dedicated to St. Margaret is now known as All Saints Church.

St. Margaret's Church, Little Staughton. Photos: Hilary and Nigel Worker

Although illiteracy was common at the time, surprisingly the marriage certificate has no signatures at all. Not only did Mary and Samuel sign with a cross, but the two witnesses, Jonathon Smith and Mary's sister Jane Pedley did the same. Like for the birth certificate, the person writing the marriage certificate (in this case probably the curate) would have needed to ask for the names and write them on behalf of the participants. This time, instead of Wadner, Mary's pronunciation must have sounded like Waddington because on the certificate both her surname and that of her father James is given as that. Since she could neither read nor write, she wouldn't have noticed the incorrect entries when she marked a cross next to where the curate pointed.

Neither Mary nor Samuel gave their actual age at the wedding, and the certificate states 'full' in the space for their age. This was fairly common practice at the time, and indicated that they were both over the age of twenty one. Perhaps the fact that Mary was thirty three and Samuel only twenty three was an embarrassment, because it was sometimes considered improper for a man to marry an older woman.

Tom's Great Grandparents Charles and Mary Smith c1870. Photo: Courtesy of Toni Bracher[10]

The 1861 census shows Mary living with Samuel Smith and Arthur aged four at Top End, Little Staughton. Arthur is recorded with the surname Smith, but when he was old enough to understand, he decided that his surname should be that of his mother's before she married. At the age of fourteen he is recorded on the next census as Arthur Wadner. Up until that point, all of his descendants starting with Tom, his brothers Frederick, Jim and Arthur Jr. and sister Rosa, would have been Smiths.

Mary was fifty four in 1881 and still married to Samuel Smith. They were living at Bushmead Cross, a small hamlet of barely half a dozen buildings about 4 miles west of Eaton Socon[11]. The hamlet stands at a crossroads about halfway between Colmworth and Little Staughton, barely a stone's throw from their cottage at Top End, Little Staughton. The dwellings have since been demolished, although a farm has sprung up in place of one of them on the northern edge of the original hamlet.

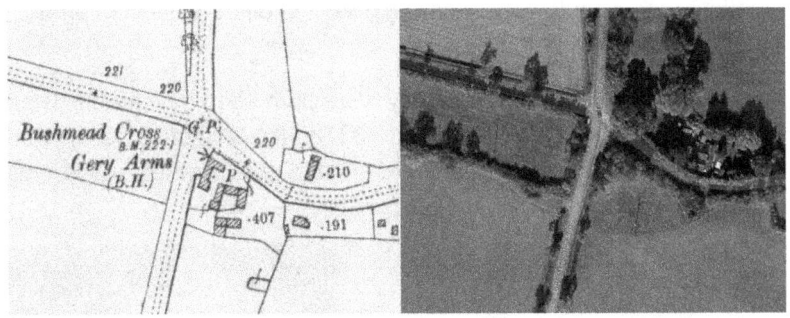

Bushmead Cross 1890 (left) vs Present Day (right). Map: National Library of Scotland

Mary died at home on the 17th April 1881. Her cause of death is given as suppurative nephritis, a type of inflammation of the kidneys which even these days is considered a serious condition. Samuel was present at her death.

Samuel, then a widower, continued to live in the same cottage by himself and made a scant living as an agricultural labourer, picking up just enough work to keep the wolf from the door. He died in 1907 when he was seventy.

Tom could not have known his grandmother Mary because she died four years before he was born. Step grandfather Samuel, though, was still alive when Tom was twenty two, and he might have regularly dropped off for a visit when he was working with his Uncle Gilbert at

Glebe Farm, just a few miles north of Bushmead Cross between Great Staughton and Grafham.

John Cade - Tom's Maternal Grandfather

John Cade was born in 1820 in Little Gransden, Cambridgeshire, to Wright Cade, an agricultural labourer, and Mary, née Newman. Wright was aged twenty six and Mary was nineteen when they were married in 1815. John's father took the given name Wright from his great grandfather's surname, William Wright (1650-1720) and was the first of four brothers and three sisters. The family lived in the parish of Great Staughton in 1841 and the census that year shows them, together with about thirty other families, under the place name of Perry to the north of the parish.

John married Alice Wise when they were both aged seventeen. Their marriage was registered in October 1837 in the district of Huntingdon and probably took place in Ellington, since that is where Alice was born. The couple lived with John's parents.

Ellington Church and Churchyard. Photos: Hilary and Nigel Worker

By 1851, John and Alice and John's brother George had moved out of the family home. George didn't go far, and lived next door with his wife Caroline and one year old daughter Harriet. John and Alice were not far away either, living just four cottages along the street with their children Thomas (12), William (5) and Mary (2).

John Cade lived in Perry for all his life and worked as an agricultural labourer. Even at the age of eighty one, and living alone, he was still occupied as an 'Ordinary Farm Labourer'. He died in 1903 at the age of eighty three.

Alice Wise - Tom's Maternal Grandmother

Alice Wise was the last of eleven children, born in 1820 in Ellington, a small village about 3 miles north of Perry and 4 miles west of Huntingdon to John Wise and Sarah, née Shelton. Her father John died the year she was born and her mother Sarah died the following year. The eldest of Alice's ten siblings was aged seventeen when she was born, so there was plenty of help available while she was growing up.

When she was seventeen, Alice married John Cade, a farm labourer from Little Gransden. She lived with John at his parent's cottage in Perry for a few years after they married, but they moved into a nearby cottage soon after their first son Thomas was born in 1839.

Between 1846 and 1865, Alice and John had five more children. William was born in 1846, Mary in 1849, Amelia in 1855, Thirza in 1862 and the youngest, Mahala, in 1865.

The names Thirza and Mahala were perhaps an unusual choice of name. Both are of Hebrew origin, have biblical connections, and are mentioned in Old Testament texts. It might be significant that they are the two youngest children in the family, which would tie in with a mounting interest in religion through the 19th century.

Alice was staying at her son William's shop at 8 St. Paul's Street in Stamford, Lincolnshire on the 6th June 1881. William, who would become Tom's uncle, was one of the first in the family to break away from agricultural labouring and had set up as a tailor and greengrocer in the town. Although requiring an unlikely combination of skills, his wife Elizabeth and eldest child Thomas probably helped out with the variety of tasks while the four youngest attended school.

8 St. Paul's Street, Stamford, present day. Photo: Google Maps, Streetview

In 1881, the bookshop shown in the photograph to the left was home to a boot-maker so was probably a shoe shop at the time. To the right was Jemima Pepper, a dressmaker. It was probably useful to find a dressmaker and tailor next to each other, although less so William's greengrocery venture.

Alice Cade still lived in Perry with her husband John when she died in 1894 at the age of seventy four. Of all their seven children, it would be Amelia and Thirza, who married Gilbert Lincoln of Grafham, who would turn out to play major roles in Tom's life.

Arthur Wadner - Tom's Father

Tom's father Arthur was born on the 21st August 1856 in Newtown, Kimbolton to the unmarried Mary Wadner, probably at Mary's family home. Although Mary's father James had died some years before in 1847, she would have been supported by her mother Sarah while Arthur was very young.

Arthur was four years old when Mary married his step father Samuel Smith in 1860, so probably remembered little of his early years in Kimbolton. His new home, Little Staughton, had a population of 572 and the male residents were almost entirely agricultural workers[12]. Many of the women earned money at lace making and it is said that there was a lace school in the village which some twelve girls attended[13]. There was also a national school which opened in 1846 on Colmworth Road towards the southern end of the village, and a Baptist chapel. Arthur would have been among about 60 children who attended the school on Sundays. The attendance dropped to about 40 during the week, probably due to many of the children working[14]. The school closed in 1983 and has since been demolished. The land on which the school and grounds once stood now contains three houses and the village hall.

Top End, Lt. Staughton 1892 (left) vs Present Day (right)[15]. Maps: National Library of Scotland

In 1948, the Bedfordshire Magazine reported that Little Staughton was known as the 'Lost Village' because during the Second World

War, some of the Top End area was demolished to make way for an aerodrome. This included twenty houses and two public houses, the Bushel and Strike and the Shoulder of Mutton.

Arthur grew up in Top End, along the sprawling line of cottages on the main road heading south from the Baptist chapel towards Bushmead Cross and Colmworth. Examining the 1861 census, the Shoulder of Mutton public house is entry number 8 and appears to mark the southern extent of Top End, and the northern end with entry number 44 is at the Baptist chapel. Arthur's cottage is entry number 40, so being closer to the village hub it might have escaped being demolished in the 1940s, although there are few old buildings around that area which remain standing now.

It wasn't every day that someone in a small rural village was convicted of murder and sentenced to death. William Bull, a twenty one year old labourer in the village, murdered Sarah Marshall on the 29th November 1870 when she was fifty one[16]. Arthur will almost certainly have known of the murder and was probably well acquainted with the perpetrator. Bull lived in the West End area near to the national school. The Bedfordshire Times carried a full report of the murder, trial and execution in the edition published on the 4th April 1871. Sarah (known locally as Old Sally) was sexually assaulted and murdered by Bull late at night in her small one-roomed cottage on the High Street. He had been drinking at Wildman's beer-house, although he did not admit to being drunk or use that to excuse his actions.

There were more than enough public houses in the village to serve the small population. Out of the ninety three dwellings, quite a few of which were uninhabited because they were run down or in danger of collapse, five were public houses. Between the Shoulder of Mutton to the south, demolished in the Second World War because of the airfield, and the Kangaroo Inn to the north, now a privately owned house, there was also The Crown, and the Bushel and Strike. Out in the West End was Edward Wildman's beer-house which is not identified as an inn at the time, but was probably the Carpenter's Arms. So, for every twenty dwellings in Little Staughton there was a public house, an unimaginable ratio these days.

Having been found guilty at trial, on the 27th March 1871 William Bull confessed to the murder, and was hanged at Bedford Prison one week later on the 3rd April at 8 a.m.

Some of the villagers will have travelled to Bedford for the hanging and Arthur, aged fourteen, might well have accompanied them. Executions were carried out in public until 1868, but a change in the law meant that in 1871 this was prohibited. The scaffold for William Bull was erected just inside the front gates of the prison, and screens were set up to prevent the hanging being witnessed from properties in the adjoining Adelaide Square. Bull was hanged by the infamous William Calcraft, who travelled up from his usual place of work at Newgate Prison in London. Calcraft retired in 1874 at the age of seventy four. In his forty five year career, he carried out some 450 executions, many of them bungled and requiring further action to ensure the condemned man was put to death[17]. In Bull's case, it was a full hour before he was taken down from the scaffold, so it seems likely that he died of strangulation rather than a broken neck. Indeed, the inquest found that he died from apoplexy caused by hanging[18].

Sarah's cottage in Little Staughton was pulled down[19].

Amelia Cade - Tom's Mother

Amelia Cade, Tom's mother, was born in Perry early in 1855 to John and Alice Cade. Her birth is registered as Biddy Amelia, and on the 1861 census for Perry she is recorded aged six as Bidda A (the enumerator misheard again). Biddy is thought to be of Irish origin, and is sometimes used as a diminutive of Bridget or Brigid. Although at the time the name was in common use, it came to be considered a derogatory term for an interfering old woman, and this might be why Amelia stopped using it.

Fourth youngest in the family, Amelia's older brother Thomas was already sixteen when she was born, with William aged nine and Mary aged six. It would be a further seven years before her younger sister Thirza arrived, and Mahala three years after that.

At the age of sixteen in 1871, Amelia was staying a few miles south of Perry in Little Staughton with her elder sister Mary. Mary had married one Thomas Smith in 1868. Living in the adjacent cottage were Samuel and Mary Smith, a coincidence of surnames, with Mary's illegitimate fourteen year old son Arthur Wadner who was working as an agricultural labourer. Although Samuel did have a brother named Thomas, two years younger than himself, it was not he who lived next door. Arthur is recorded on the census form as 'son-in-law', although these days we would understand his relationship to the head of the household to be 'step-son'. It was usual in the 19th century to refer to a child who was born out of wedlock using the mother's maiden name, but afford the child the legal status of a son through 'son-in-law'[20].

Schedule	Road, Street	Houses	Name and Surname	Relation to Head of Family	Condition	Age M	Age F	Profession	Birth
32		1	Thomas Smith	Head	Married	23		Ag Lab	Beds Lt Staughton
			Mary ditto	Wife	Married		22		Hunts Perry
			Amelia Cade	Visitor	+		16		ditto
			Juliana Smith	Daugh	+		11 weeks		Beds Lt Staughton
33		1	Samuel Smith	Head	Married	34		Ag Lab	ditto
			Mary ditto	Wife	Married		41		Hunts Kimbolton
			Arthur Wadner	Son in law	+	14			ditto

Transcription from 1871 Census for Little Staughton

We can only speculate why Amelia was staying at her sister's house, but it seems as though she and Arthur took a shine to each other over the garden fence. Three years later, in 1874, Arthur Wadner married Amelia Cade, the girl next door who he had known since he was fourteen years old.

Arthur and Amelia - Tom's Parents

Arthur Wadner married Amelia Cade in St. Andrew's, Great Staughton Parish Church, on Thursday the 5th November 1874. Arthur was eighteen, and Amelia nineteen. The spaces for Arthur's father's name and occupation are left blank on his marriage certificate, so presumably his mother Mary hadn't told him the identity of his father even at that major milestone in his life.

A few years earlier, the wedding would have clashed with an annual celebration of thanks. Until 1859, all parish churches were required to hold services on the 5th November to celebrate Parliament being saved from being blown up by Guy Fawkes in the Gunpowder Plot of 1605[21]. This was known as the Observance of 5th November Act 1605 and was passed into law in 1606. Although for many years the date was also declared a public holiday, by the 1800s it had been relegated to a day of observance only[22].

St. Andrews, Great Staughton Parish Church. Photos: Hilary and Nigel Worker

It is likely that the weather on the couple's wedding day was wet and windy. 1874 was the first of the wettest ten years ever recorded up until 2009. In the few weeks either side of the wedding, there were violent gales in some parts of the country with boats being driven ashore, and extreme wind damage inland with some loss of life.

As was usually the case in small villages, the marriage certificate doesn't include residential addresses, but it does state that both Amelia and Arthur were living in Great Staughton. Three years earlier, they were teenagers in neighbouring cottages in Little Staughton. Sometime between 1871 and 1881, Arthur's mother Mary and step father Samuel Smith moved from Little Staughton to a small cottage a few hundred yards south in Bushmead Cross, and Arthur had left the family home. Amelia's family, though, were still in Great Staughton so there seems a strong possibility that Amelia was living at with them at the time of her marriage. Most of her siblings had fledged the nest by then, with just the youngest sisters Thirza and Mahala remaining. There would have been plenty of room, and there is a good chance that Arthur was living there too in the weeks and months before the wedding.

The Highway, Great Staughton, pre-1900. Photo: Great Staughton Village Website[23]

Seven years after their marriage, Arthur and Amelia moved to a cottage owned by Mount Pleasant Farm near Bolnhurst, a village not far from Bedford with sixty nine houses and a population of 279.

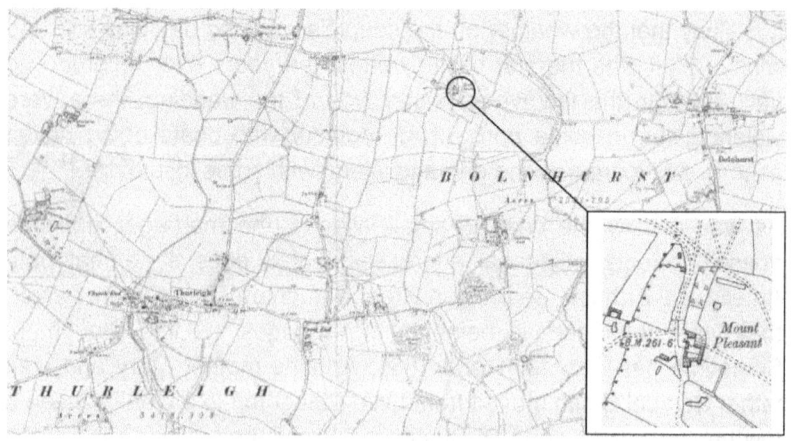

Mount Pleasant Farm near Bolnhurst. Map: National Library of Scotland

The farm was leased by Samuel Green, who worked some 250 acres and employed six men and three boys. There were three farm cottages about halfway between Bolnhurst and Thurleigh and Arthur lived in one of them with Amelia and their children Rosa Ellen, Jim, Arthur Jr. and Tom.

Goldington Highfields

Around 1887, Arthur and his family moved from Mount Pleasant to a cottage in Goldington Highfields close to where Arthur was horse keeper at Highfield Farm near Ravensden.

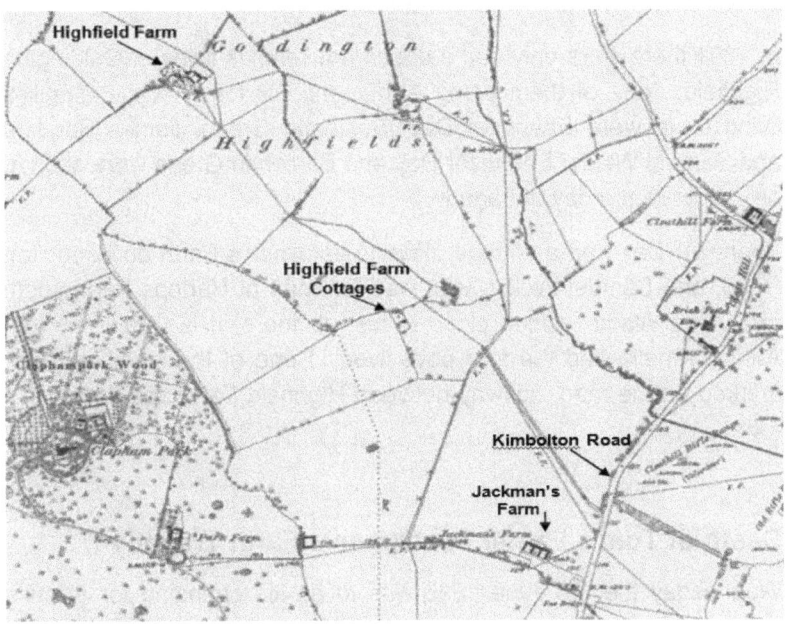

Goldington Highfields, 1884. Map: National Library of Scotland[24]

A 1932 sales brochure for the farm mentions the cottages on the schedule. It gives their area as 1 rood and 22 poles, which works out to approximately three quarters of an acre. They are difficult to see on the map, but there appear to be three cottages on the site.

Highfield Farm is quoted as having cattle yards, an orchard and pasture of about 102 acres, and about 62 acres of arable land. That suggests a mixed farm involved in cattle and perhaps sheep grazing, as well as crop growing.

Goldington Highfields was a sprawling district close to Bedford, difficult to describe precisely. Very approximately, it stretched from as far as Graze Hill near Ravensden in the north and east, arguably to the south side of Goldington Road, and bordered Clapham to the west. The southern area was certainly known as Highfields at the time of the Domesday Book where it is described as a small hamlet of eight households, but it is possible that by the nineteenth century the area didn't extend that far to the south.

In 1891 there were only half a dozen households living at Goldington Highfields, one of them being Arthur and his family. Other families living there were Ebenezer Day, Benjamin Green, James Sanders and Samuel Welch. Ebenezer Day and Benjamin Green were soon to be involved in a day of tragedy.

Ebenezer Day had a cottage close to Jackman's Farm on Kimbolton Road, and Samuel Welch, who was foreman at Hartops Farm south of Putnoe Wood resided close to his job there. It is very likely that Arthur, Amelia and the four boys lived in one of the small cottages marked on the map, halfway between Highfield Farm and Jackman's Farm.

Death of Tom's Father - Jackman's Farm Tragedy

Wednesday the 3rd June 1896 was to be life changing for Arthur's family. Tom, who would have turned eleven years old in March of that year, would have walked to school as usual. His father would almost certainly have left for work much earlier, because horse keepers were expected to be on the farm by 4:30 in the morning to make sure their charges were fed and prepared to begin work[25]. By noon, Arthur would be unconscious at Jackman's Farm, and would die the following day at around six o'clock in the evening.

Jackman's Farm 1900 (left) vs Present Day (right). Maps: National Library of Scotland

There were various accounts in the local newspapers of what happened, with headlines such as: 'The Cesspit Fatality'; 'Accident Near Bedford - Overcome by Sewer Gas'; 'Bedford - Shocking Cesspool Fatality'; and 'Poisoned by Cesspit Gas - Three Men in Danger'. Each account is different in some respects, and two appear to contradict each other regarding the sequence of events. Fortunately, the inquest two days later provides an accurate record.

The inquest was held at Jackman's Farm on Friday the 5th June in the afternoon before the County Coroner Mark Whyley, with a jury sworn in comprising Messrs. T.J. Davies (foreman), W. Ell, G. Ballinghall, T. Howkins, C. Gillett, L. Armstrong, W. Keech, J. Wootton, A. Harlow, H. Danse, F. Clark, J. Denton, and A. Day. Before the proceedings began, the jury viewed Arthur's body in the coach-house, and also inspected the scene of the tragedy.

A second man, Lumbis, was involved in the accident. None of the accounts mention Lumbis' first name, but the 1891 census for Ravensden records a Lumbis family living at 52 Cross Roads, Ravensden. The head, John Lumbis aged forty five, is recorded as a Brickmaker (as are many others in the village), while two of his sons, Arthur (16), and William (14) are recorded as Farm Labourers. The 1901 census does not mention either of these sons, but Arthur Lumbis is on the 1911 census living at 25 Newnham Lane carrying out the profession of Jobbing Gardener. There is a large brickworks shown across the road from The Polhill Arms public house at Salph

End, and it is probable that the head of the household John Lumbis was employed there. So, it is a fair guess that the man involved in the accident is likely to have been his son Arthur Lumbis, who was aged twenty one in 1896.

The evidence of an eye-witness at the inquest stated that he, Ebenezer Day, who lived at the cottage adjoining Jackman's Farm farmhouse, heard Arthur Wadner calling from the top of the cesspit tank on Wednesday the 3rd June about eleven o'clock in the morning. Arthur shouted, 'Eben, come here, quick!' As soon as Ebenezer arrived at the tank, Arthur climbed down a ladder into the tank with the rope they used for pulling a bucket up and down. Lumbis was at the bottom of the tank. When Arthur got to the bottom, he said, 'Eben, I can't...' then fell back and didn't stir.

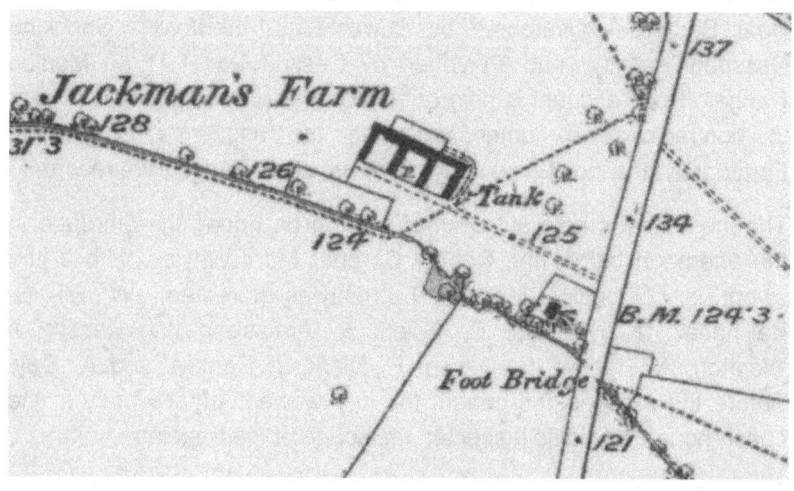

Jackman's Farm Showing Tank, 1884. Map: National Library of Scotland[26]

Benjamin Green was hoeing in a field about 200 yards away and heard somebody shout out, 'Green!' When he arrived at the tank, John Walker, the occupier of Jackman's Farm and Highfields Farm, was there with Ebenezer Day. It transpired that John Walker had asked Arthur to help Lumbis clean out the tank. Benjamin climbed down into the tank and managed to grab Arthur's collar, but it broke. Benjamin then began to feel ill, and said, 'A mist came before me so that I could not see at all...' He managed to climb back up the ladder, and Ebenezer Day and John Walker helped him out of the top. After he recovered a little, John Walker asked Benjamin to ride into Bedford and fetch a doctor. The two unconscious men were eventually pulled from the tank using a rope, and were out by the time Benjamin and the doctor, Dr. Lloyde, arrived.

Lumbis regained consciousness about two o'clock in the afternoon, and was sent home. The doctor tried everything to bring Arthur round, and visited him many times throughout the afternoon and during the night, but he died the following day about four thirty in the afternoon.

Although the entrance to the tank should have been uncovered the day before to release the poisonous gas, the inquest returned a verdict of Accidental Death from breathing carbonic acid gas.

A letter to the Bedfordshire Times and Independent on Saturday 13th June, 1896 [27] reads:

Sir, - Will you kindly allow us through the medium of your columns to call the attention of the public to a subscription now being taken in aid of the widow and family of the late A. Wadner, who so nobly lost his life in the endeavour to save that of his fellow workman under such perilous circumstances. Subscriptions will be thankfully acknowledged by Col. Warner, Ravensden; Mr. F Hughes, Lion Hotel, Bedford; and W. Mead, jun., Ravensden.

Subscription Call for Arthur Wadner's Family. Cutting: Bedfordshire Times and Independent

It has not been possible to find out how much was subscribed, because no further updates were published.

Arthur Wadner was buried at Goldington Church on Saturday the 6th June, 1896. There is no gravestone indicating where he lies. There are many explanations why that should be. Possibly, the family could not afford one. Even though Arthur would have been relatively well paid compared to farm day-workers, money will still have been short. He might even have had a pauper's burial, and pauper's graves were not generally marked with a headstone.

Given the circumstances of Arthur's death, though, he would surely have been held in high esteem for attempting to save the life of Arthur Lumbis. It seems unlikely that he would have been laid to rest without a grave marker of some kind, so there is a good probability that his gravestone has somehow been lost. Perhaps it was knocked over, placed against a wall, or crumbled over time (probably least likely as it has only been 120 years or so since his burial).

There is a distinct possibility that the gravestone was damaged in the mid-1950s, when the aisle to the north of the church, and organ chamber and vestries to the east, were demolished to make way for a new extension to the north (left of the tower as viewed from Church Lane). This was to provide a substantial increase in the floor area of the church, needed because of the population explosion in Bedford around that period. Goldington did not escape the new housing developments which sprang up to accommodate the growing number of residents. At the turn of the 20th century, some 35,000 people lived in the town but by the end of the century the population had more than doubled to 74,000.

Although there is nothing left to mark where Arthur lies, there are clues. The burial register shows the names of those interred at around the same time, and some of those still have a gravestone. Jessie Brace, Sophia Day, Ann Day and William Armstrong lie in the north-western corner of the churchyard. Looking at the reference numbers in the register, Arthur's burial on the 6th June took place between Ann Day's on the 3rd June, and William Armstrong's on the 28th July, all in 1896. This is pure speculation, but it seems likely that Arthur might be buried in the vicinity of the areas shown in photographs 1 or 3.

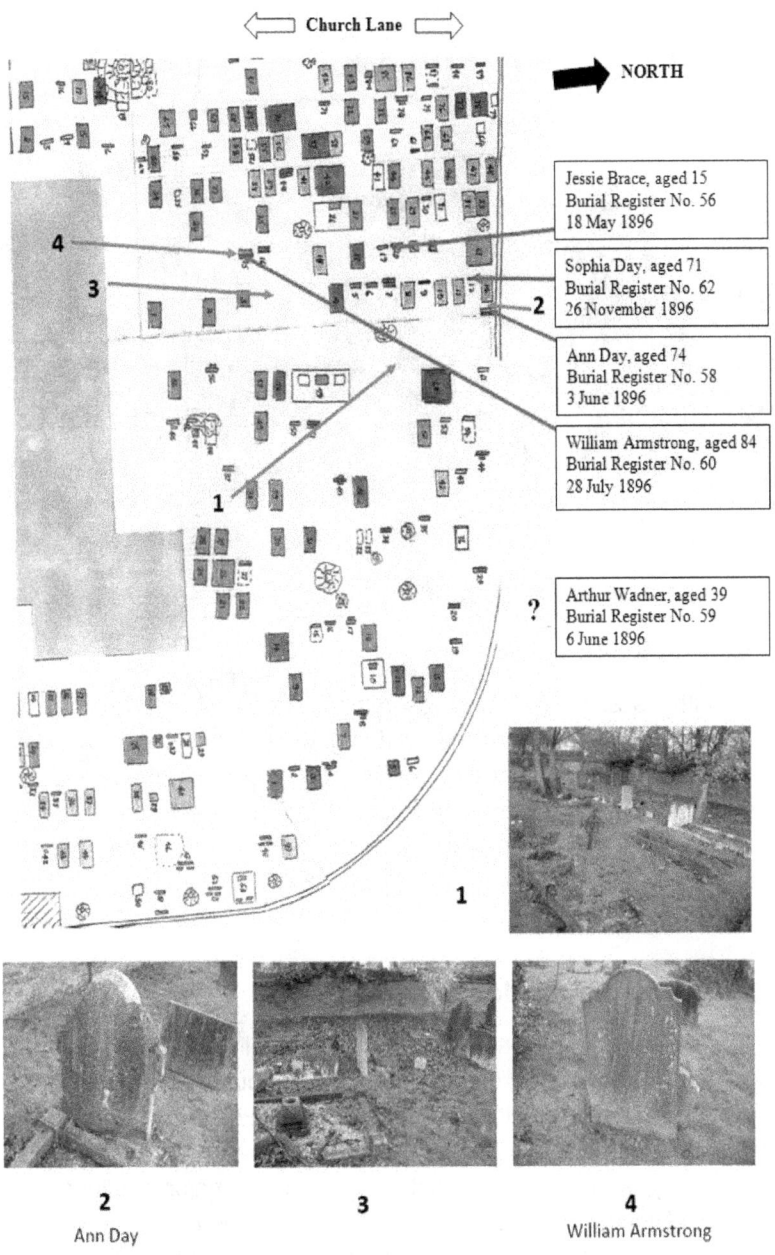

Arthur Wadner - Burial at St. Mary's Church, Goldington. Courtesy of St. Mary's Archivist

St. Mary's Church, Goldington Graveyard. Photo: © Carl Jones[28]

The author's sister Patricia was married at St. Mary's on the 2nd August, 1975. Present at the wedding were Arthur's grandchildren John, Peter, David, Betty and Joy and none of them mentioned that their grandfather was buried only yards from where they congregated. The only reasonable conclusion that can be reached, is that none of them knew.

Amelia and Jimmy Jones

Following Arthur's untimely death in 1896, Amelia will almost certainly have had to leave their cottage because it would have been tied to her husband's job as Horse-keeper at Highfield Farm. Working out what to do with the children still living at home, Fred (9), Tom (11), Arthur (14), and Jim (18) must have been a major challenge for Amelia. Although Bedfordshire was well known for its cottage industries, such as lace-making, there are no records which indicate that Amelia had any craft skills. The family would have relied totally on Arthur's wages for income and on his job to provide their home.

Amelia re-married four years after Arthur's death, at Ravensden Parish Church on the 4th October 1900, the seventh of only eight marriages celebrated that year[29]. Her new husband was James Jones (referred to by his step grandchildren as 'Old Jimmy Jones'), a farmer and brick merchant, although the parish record shows him simply as 'Brickmaker'. His first wife Sarah died at the age of 52 on the 10th August 1899, fourteen months before he married Amelia.

Sarah Jones' Gravestone - Ravensden Church. Photo: Jacquie Sullivan[30]

Jimmy Jones was born in 1845 in the hamlet of Honeydon, about three miles west of Eaton Socon, to an agricultural labourer. He moved to Ravensden in 1860 at the age of fifteen to become a servant to Daniel and Christina Colbert next door to the White Lion on Kimbolton Road. By 1871 he was working as an agricultural labourer and living a couple of doors away from the chapel on Oldway Road, behind which stood the cottage where he was to spend the rest of his life. Jimmy is recorded variously as a grocer and farmer of 12 acres and as an employer, and a brick merchant.

The thought that Jimmy re-married so quickly, and had to pass so very close to his deceased wife's grave to do so, seems rather strange in modern times. However, there was not the choice of wedding venue that there is now, and the marriage would have had to take place in the parish of Ravensden. It is doubtful that Sarah would have minded anyway. Looking at cold facts, Jimmy needed someone to help care for his children who were still living at home, and Amelia, for her part, needed a roof over her head.

Jimmy Jones was ten years older than Amelia, and had nine children with Sarah, who he had married in 1867. William was their first, born in 1869 and he and Ruth, Albert, Jabez and Ann had left home by the time Jimmy and Amelia married. That left Henry (19), Charles (18), Christiana (14) and Emily (10) to share their cottage. There was no room for Amelia's children, and they had to make their own way from that point on.

Driving through Ravensden village, it would be very easy to miss Jimmy and Amelia's cottage on Oldway Road. The family home was set back behind the Baptist Chapel, and the three cottages in Chapel Yard accessed via Chapel Lane, a hundred yards or so along from what is now known as Ravensden Crossroads.

It appears that Jimmy's '12 acres' might have been between Ravensden and Renhold. Although it is not clear exactly what use Jimmy made of his land, there were numerous reports in the local newspapers which mention him. For instance, on the 14th November 1902 Charles Cook, a baker, and John Allen, a fishmonger, were summonsed for trespassing in search of game in one of Jimmy's fields[31]. Also, on the 5th February 1904, one Thomas Rabbit was summonsed for trespassing 'in search of conies' on Jimmy's land at Renhold[32]. Suspiciously appearing to be a case of a false identity being given by the accused (a cony usually referred to a rabbit), the prosecuting superintendant was 'anxious for the case to be withdrawn' and this was granted.

Jimmy might even have had some sheep in 1902, because he appeared on the 19th June that year at Bedford County Court in front of Judge Shortt, to lodge a claim against one Colonel Sunderland of Ravensden for shooting his stock dog[33]. The report states that Jimmy was a long-term occupier of land in Ravensden. Sunderland said he shot the dog when he saw it chasing a rabbit on his land. Jimmy was claiming £4 in compensation, but witnesses responded that the dog was a brindle collie cross and only worth five shillings at the most. The judge settled on something in between and ordered Sanderson to pay Jimmy two guineas and pay costs.

Jimmy and Amelia certainly had a cow. On the 18th March 1921, they were accused of selling milk deficient in fat[34]. One H. James paid Amelia 4d for a pint of milk, which was found to have less milk fat than it should have contained, suggesting that it had been watered down. Amelia claimed that she told the purchaser that they only had one cow, which was 'not as good as the one they had before' and that the milk had come directly from the cow. The case against them was dismissed.

The photograph of Amelia (over) shows her seated in a field with houses behind her. She appears to be aged around sixty five, which would date the photograph around 1920. There were no houses like those in the background where she lived in Ravensden, but it is possible she was visiting her son and Tom's older brother, Jim. Jim lived at London Row on Clapham High Street at that time, and the chimneys on the roofs appear to match the houses as they are today. About twenty yards to Amelia's left would be the River Ouse, and she could have been enjoying a peaceful afternoon at the riverbank.

Amelia Cade in Later Years. Photo: Courtesy of Bob Webber

Jimmy Jones was 80 when he died at their home in Ravensden on the 23rd August 1926. He was suffering from senile decay. Jimmy's funeral was reported in the Bedfordshire Times as taking place at All Saints Church, Ravensden on the 24th August 1926, although the burial register entry is dated the 25th August, and is probably the correct date. Although Amelia attended the funeral, notably absent were any of her children or grandchildren. It is understandable that they might have carried a life-long grudge after having nowhere to live after Amelia's decision to move in with Jimmy and his own children following their marriage. Neither did the large number of wreaths include any from Rosa, Fred or Jim although one was sent 'In affectionate remembrance' from Tom and his wife.

After Jimmy's death, Amelia continued to live at Chapel Yard with Jimmy's son Albert and daughter-in-law Mary Ann until 1938. After becoming seriously ill, she moved in with Tom at 4 Dudley Street, Bedford. Tom was present at his mother's death on the 26th December 1938. She was 83 years old, and died from stomach cancer. Amelia's funeral was held at All Saints Church, Ravensden on the 30th December. Both Rosa and Jim had passed on before their mother, but wreaths were sent from Tom and Violet, and Fred and his wife Ada in Bristol, as well as tributes from her grandchildren.

The Early Years

Tom was born on the 17th March 1885, and was Arthur and Amelia's fourth child after Rosa, Jim and Arthur Jr.

His siblings' birth certificates show that they were born in Bolnhurst, but Tom's place of birth is given as Thurleigh. This is a puzzle, because although Arthur Jr. was baptised in Thurleigh at St. Peter's Church, if Tom really was born in the village he was the odd one out.

The most probable explanation is that a mistake was made when Amelia registered Tom's birth nearly six weeks later on the 27th April 1885. She was very close to the 42 day deadline for informing the authorities, and might have hurriedly said 'Thurleigh' without giving it much thought. After all, the labourer's cottages at Mount Pleasant Farm, where Tom's father Arthur worked, are almost mid-point between Bolnhurst and Thurleigh and it would have been an easy slip-up.

Although we have to take the birth certificate entry of Thurleigh as correct, official documents were often prone to errors and it is most likely that Tom was actually born in the same farm cottage as his siblings.

By the time Tom was two years old, his father had moved from his job at Mount Pleasant Farm to work at Highfield Farm near Ravensden as horse keeper, and the family was living at Goldington Highfields.

School

Judging by the number of entries on marriage and birth certificates in the family that carry a mark instead of a signature, it would be fair to say that many of Tom's ancestors had little or no schooling. This wasn't unusual in the late 18th and early 19th centuries, especially in agricultural counties such as Bedfordshire. You didn't need to read or write to cut hay, pull vegetables or harvest cereal crops.

By the mid 1800s there was a drive to educate working class children to prepare them better for the industrialisation of working practices which was taking place. Religious groups began to establish schools throughout England funded by voluntary contributions from the local community. At first, these were mostly Sunday schools to avoid a clash between education and work, but in 1870 an Education Act was passed to provide for the setting up of school boards funded by local authorities.

A Record of Service sheet from The National Archives army records has a hand-written entry showing that Tom was educated at Goldington Board School in Bedford.

Goldington School, 1905. Photo: Courtesy of John Wainwright[35]

Although there is some conflicting data, it appears that the original National School was built in 1865 at a cost of £1400 which was raised by subscription from the local community. The school was designed to accommodate 174 children of both sexes, with an annex attached for the head master. The name was changed to Goldington Board School in 1872, and the Jubilee Clock, also paid for by local subscription, was added in 1887 to celebrate the Golden Jubilee of Queen Victoria. The bell stopped chiming in World War Two and has never worked since. In 1903 the name of the school was changed yet again, this time to Goldington Council School, and since 1946 there have been other variations. It is most recently known as Goldington Green Academy.

The census taken on the night of the 5th April 1891 records Tom at the age of six as a scholar. His brother Fred was three years younger so not yet at school and, strangely, Arthur Jr. who was nine has a blank where the enumerator might have written scholar. Jim, the eldest brother aged thirteen, has his occupation as agricultural labourer, the same as his father Arthur.

Rosa would have attended Bolnhurst church school around 1881 when she was five years old. It was closed after two years to build an extension, increasing the schoolroom dimensions to about thirty by fifteen feet which was judged sufficient to accommodate 62 pupils[36]. The school reopened as a board school in 1885, but less than twenty years later a 1904 survey was scathing about the condition of the playground, which was described as 'filthy and dangerous', and the water supply whose rainwater filter had been 'stirred up' as causing a 'very serious source of contamination'. By 1913 the attendance had dwindled to 27. An inspection in 1925 noted that the building was cold (the schoolroom was heated by an open fire), and that the cesspits were not emptied frequently enough. In spite of the building attracting adverse description, the quality of work by the pupils was judged 'remarkable'. Attendance at the school had fallen to 10 by 1938, and it was closed in 1950. The four remaining pupils transferred to Keysoe School[37].

In 1883, Rosa moved to Thurleigh Free School until she was ten. She was described as 'very backward'[38] even though she was a year older than Jim. Jim is recorded as being admitted to the Thurleigh Free/Lower School at the age of five on the 13th October 1883.

Jim and Rosa moved on to Clapham Parochial/Ursula Taylor School on the 21st April 1886 after the family moved to Goldington Highfields, but are shown as having withdrawn on the 24th September that same year. Rosa was re-admitted in November and finally withdrew on the 28th January 1887 at the age of eleven. They were not to know that over 100 years later, their great niece and the author's sister Patricia (1953-2000) would be at that same school, albeit the rebuilt Ursula Taylor, cooking and serving dinners to the children.

The Goldington Board School logbook covering 1887-1901 shows Tom was admitted from Highfields Goldington on Tuesday the 15th April 1890 at the age of five and withdrew on Thursday the 17th March 1898 on his thirteenth birthday. The log book also records Fred being admitted on the 10th April 1893 and leaving on the 17th September 1900 at thirteen. Tom's older brother Jim was too old to be a pupil at Goldington Board School after the family moved from Mount Pleasant.

Arthur Jr. is shown starting on the 13th June 1892, which explains why the census does not show him as a scholar in 1891. It wasn't immediately clear why he didn't attend until he was so much older, until reading the school log book entry. It reads, 'Admitted Arthur Wadner from Goldington Highfields. He is 10 years old, and is a cripple, and has never been to school before.' Arthur is recorded as leaving the school on the 26th April 1897 at the age of fifteen. Both Tom and Fred have their reason for leaving noted as 'Age. Farm Labourer'. No reason is given for Arthur, but by fifteen he was older than the expected leaving age.

An entry in the logbook for the 1st March 1895 (Tom would have been 10 years old) reads, 'Punished Thomas Wadner for impudence to the Pupil Teacher and for attempting to kick her.' He probably wasn't the only spirited pupil in the school and the teacher was not without being admonished. On the 10th May 1892, the headmaster Lewis T. White wrote in the logbook, 'Cautioned the Pupil Teacher to be more careful in marking the registers, so as to avoid blots and smears.'

It appears from other entries in the logbook that there were about 100 pupils attending the school. In May 1892 the average varied between 103 and 109 and 'two cases of mumps' were noted. In March 1895, the attendance average was stated to be between 94 and 90 but there were 'some fresh cases of mumps' and 'some cases of influenza' which might have affected attendance. This could have been Russian Flu, because between November 1891 and June 1892, a second outbreak of that strain killed about a million people worldwide[39].

It seems odd that there is no entry in the school log for Tom, Fred or Arthur Jr. around 3rd June 1896 when their father was killed in the cess tank accident. Maybe they just attended school as normal, or perhaps accidental death was more common then and unworthy of any special attention.

Sadly, this photograph of pupils at Goldington School doesn't include Tom or his brothers, but they could have known some of them.

Class from Goldington School c1900. Photo: Unknown

Judging by the dress code, the photograph was probably taken around the turn of the century although it was traditional for boys to wear Eton starched collars and the girls pinafores even back to the 1860s[40] so it could be earlier.

It appears that Tom was fairly quick on his feet, because on the 8th March 1898 the school board arranged races on Goldington Green. Tom made it through the heats to the finals, but was out-run by others in his class[41]. That must have been one of the last school activities he took part in before leaving.

Although the teaching was probably limited to reading, writing and arithmetic with little time for self-expression, Tom left school at the age of thirteen with all the skills needed to make a success of his army career which was waiting around the corner.

Glebe Farm

After his mother Amelia re-married and moved in with Jimmy Jones in 1900, at the age of fourteen Tom needed somewhere to stay. He left home to help out at Glebe Farm, Grafham, living with his uncle and aunt Gilbert and Thirza Lincoln at Glebe Farm Cottage. Thirza was Amelia's younger sister. Tom is recorded in the 1901 census as Gilbert's nephew employed as an agricultural labourer. Gilbert is shown as 'Horsekeeper Man on Farm', and Tom's cousin William Lincoln (8) also lived at the cottage. The farm was almost exactly halfway between Grafham and East Perry and about one mile from each village.

Gilbert had married Thirza at Great Staughton Church on the 17th May 1880 when she was twenty, and they lived in Perry with Thirza's father John Cade. The 1881 census shows Gilbert as 'Son-in-law and lodger', and also records two children as John Cade's grandchildren, Joseph W. Cade aged three, and James Lincoln aged one month.

Glebe Farm, Grafham. Photo: Courtesy of Colin Brett and Stephen Ellerbeck

In the 1880s, Glebe Farm was about 300 acres, of which 80 acres were grass[42]. The Bedfordshire Times carried an advertisement in

1950 for a cowman to work at Glebe Farm with the Friesian herd, and offered an excellent cottage with bathroom and water situated on the road near the village. A 1920s map of the area shows a group of two or three cottages near to the farm on Church Hill, and one of these was probably Glebe Farm Cottage. Crops grown on the surviving farms around the area in the present day include wheat, barley and rape. There wouldn't have been a market for rape in 1901, so it is likely that wheat and barley would have been the major crops.

A 1960 Ordnance Survey map shows that Glebe Farm had changed its name to Rectory Farm, but that didn't save it from the fate that was to befall it together with other buildings in the vicinity. The area was submerged under Grafham Water in 1965. The farmhouse was left intact under the water, but the cottages were demolished before the area was flooded, to make the area safer for fishing and water sports.

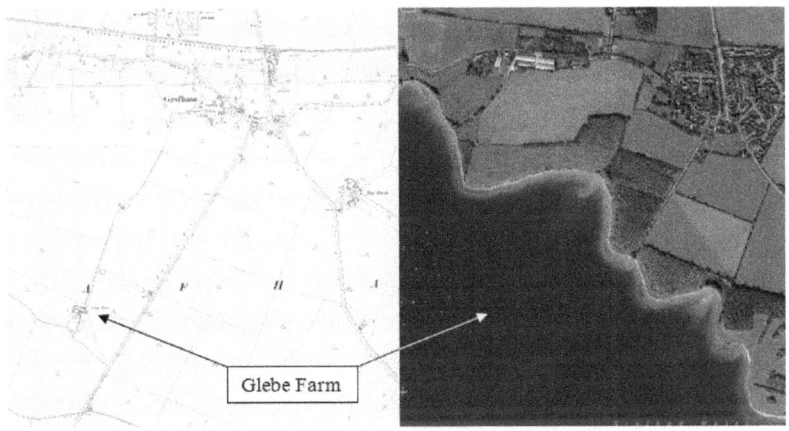

Glebe Farm then (left) and now (right). Image: National Library of Scotland

The author and his sister Patricia were photographed standing on the dam at the eastern edge of the reservoir in the early 1960s. Construction was started in 1962, but it would be four years before the reservoir was full. Nothing was mentioned either at the time the photograph was taken, or later, that the farm Tom had worked on when he was sixteen was underneath the water just a few hundred yards from where his grandson and granddaughter stood. Perhaps none of his children knew.

Author and sister Patricia, Grafham Water Dam c1964. Photo: Author

Grafham Water was created in 1965 to keep up with the demands of a growing Bedfordshire and Northamptonshire population, as well as the demand from the new town at Milton Keynes. It was initially known as Diddington Reservoir after the brook whose valley it flooded, and is filled from the River Ouse. Surface area of the reservoir is about 1500 acres, its circumference about 10 miles and capacity about 57.8 million cubic metres[43].

Grafham Water 2017. Photo: Hilary and Nigel Worker

The Rose Inn

It is not possible to say how long Tom worked at Glebe Farm with his uncle, but he later moved back to Goldington and gave that as his address when he joined the army in 1904. For at least some of that time between the ages of sixteen and nineteen, Tom worked as a groom at The Rose public house at 45 High Street, Bedford.

The Rose, Bedford, Now and c1950. Photos: Google Maps, Streetview (left) and Unknown (right)

The Rose is one of the oldest inns in Bedford and is thought to date back to the 16th century, although the present frontage is the result of improvements implemented in 1836[44]. At the time Tom worked there, the inn was run under the name of Morris & Company, a local brewer based in Church Street, Ampthill. As a business, Morris & Company had collapsed in 1858 and was taken over by John Thomas Green of Woburn, although the old name was retained until 1926[45].

By the 1920s, horse drawn vehicles had all but disappeared from the streets of Bedford and been replaced by motor cars, but only twenty years earlier they were the main form of transport.

Carriages (left) near The Rose, Bedford High Street c1900. Photo: Unknown

Tom would have been responsible for the horses after they had arrived at the inn, ensuring they were fed and watered and had sufficient bedding. He would also have checked that their tack was clean and in good condition and that the horse and carriage was ready to resume its journey when the owner required it.

Tom at The Rose Public House, c1903. Photo: Courtesy of Clinton Blackburn

Compared to the wages of an agricultural labourer, Tom would have been handsomely paid at a rate of around a guinea each week, and could have expected tips on top of that, perhaps between a shilling and half a crown depending upon the service given[46]. His employer would also have supplied a set of suitable stable clothes every six months or so, and the photograph of Tom at The Rose shows him smartly dressed in waistcoat, breeches, leggings and boots.

It was not unusual for a groom to live in at his place of work, and Tom could well have been boarding at The Rose. It was only about a year later that he and his brother Fred joined the army. Tom's enlistment document shows his address as the Parish of Goldington, and Fred's shows the same. This poses an interesting question though: Where exactly were the brothers living when they joined up?

In 1904, their mother Amelia was in Ravensden with her new husband Jimmy Jones, sister Rosa was married and living in Bradwell (now part of Milton Keynes), and brother Jim and his wife were in Bromham, near Bedford. Fred had been living with Rosa and her husband Stephen Odell in Bradwell since the age of thirteen. None of these locations is anywhere near Goldington, so it is possible that in 1904 Tom and Fred were lodging there together. There were members of the Odell family living in Chapel Yard, Goldington in 1891 who are recorded as having boarders. Odell family members were still living there in 1924 so the brothers could well have been staying with them when they joined up. Chapel Yard is no longer there, but it ran approximately alongside the modern extension to the left of Goldington School viewed from Goldington Green. There were also Odells living at 7 Alexandra Road, Goldington in 1911 so Tom and Fred could have been staying there.

This is all conjecture though, and the brothers might not have been staying at the same location. They might simply have agreed to quote 'Parish of Goldington' as their address on enlistment.

Army Service

The second Boer War of 1899-1902 resulted in the death of some 22,000 British officers and men, and left 23,000 injured or captured. Diseases such as dysentery and typhoid fever accounted for another 12,000 deaths. Most regiments of the army were involved in the war, including the Bedfordshire Regiment whose 2nd Battalion arrived at the Cape, South Africa, by sea on the 8th January 1900. The British Army was greatly depleted and needed to enlist thousands more men, particularly faced with strong industrialised nations such as Germany who could easily challenge for supremacy over Britain[47].

Tom and Fred both signed up for the British Army on the 21st January 1904. Fred would have been sixteen and lied about his age. His army record shows his birthday as the 20th January 1886, but it was actually the 20th August 1887. To join the British Army, applicants had to be eighteen years of age, and nineteen to be eligible for overseas duties. Presumably this is why there was some creativity surrounding Tom's and Fred's actual birthdays.

Tom had turned eighteen in June of the previous year but gave his birthday as the 21st December 1884, which made him nineteen years and one month. He was actually born three months later, on the 15th March, 1885. This little white lie would eventually catch him out, when he tried to claim his army pension three months too early.

It was quite easy at the time to lie about one's age, because although births were registered, very few people actually had possession of their birth certificates. The practice was tightened up after one John Condon was killed at the 2nd battle of Ypres in 1916 at the age of fourteen. National Registration was introduced soon after, and all adults were required to have identity cards[48].

The brothers were recruited at Bedford on Thursday the 21st January 1904, and both requested to join the 1st Battalion of the Kings Royal Rifle Corps. It is surprising that the Bedfordshire Regiment was not their first choice, especially as they almost certainly would have been running a recruitment campaign at Kempston Barracks near Bedford. However, the KRRC was involved in the high profile Boer War fighting at Talana Hill, the first battle of the war, and at Waggon Hill during the relief of Ladysmith. Tom and Fred would have been exposed to the progress of the war through the popular press, which reported every event in great detail[49]. Added to this, in the early 1900s the British Empire was climbing towards its peak, with direct influence over some 412 million people and a quarter of the Earth's land area[50]. A combination of national pride, a widespread expectation that young men would pursue a military career and the attraction of prestigious regiments such as the KRRC probably fuelled the brother's desire to join up. It would only have taken a local KRRC recruitment drive, perhaps even taking place at The Rose where Tom worked, or at the nearby marketplace a few yards along Bedford's High Street, to clinch their decision to embark upon a military career.

Fred completed attestation immediately before Tom. His service number was 5879 and Tom's was 5880. After their attestation was signed off, the brothers were subjected to a medical examination and Tom came through with no problems apart from a bad tooth. Height 5 feet 5 inches, weight 140 pounds (10 stones exactly), chest measurement 36 inches and physical development 'Very Good'. Five years of agricultural labouring since leaving school had ensured he was in good shape for an army career. He was described as of fresh complexion, with pale grey eyes and dark brown hair. The only distinctive marks recorded were burn scars above, below, and behind the left knee joint. The average height of a recruit at the time was around 5 feet 5 inches so Tom was spot on, but his weight was well above the average of 8 stones[51]. Most young men of that time were undernourished, and at 8½ stones with a chest measurement of 31 inches Fred was much nearer the average, perhaps because he was more than two years younger than his brother.

The brothers would have been given a day's pay of one shilling after attestation and instructed to report to their regiment. The 21st January 1904 was a Thursday, and their travel warrant and joining instructions would have taken a day or two to arrive. Tom joined the Kings Royal Rifle Corps 1st Battalion at Gosport, near Southampton, on the following Monday the 25th January 1904 for early training in the rank of Rifleman.

Tom in Walking Out Uniform[52] 1906. Photo: Courtesy of Carol Cannell

The photograph of Tom shows him in his undress, walking out uniform. The tunic was a very dark rifle green, and the KRRC version was marked by a line of scarlet piping running along the base of the collar and a similar line tracing the black inverted chevron decoration on the cuff. The cuff decoration signifies his Good Conduct Badge which he earned on the 21st January 1906. Tom was promoted to lance corporal on the 11th April 1906, and as there are no stripes on his uniform it is possible to date the photograph with some accuracy as being taken between those dates. The swagger stick is a red herring. Although often thought to be something only officers carried, before WW1 it was available to all ranks including rifleman.

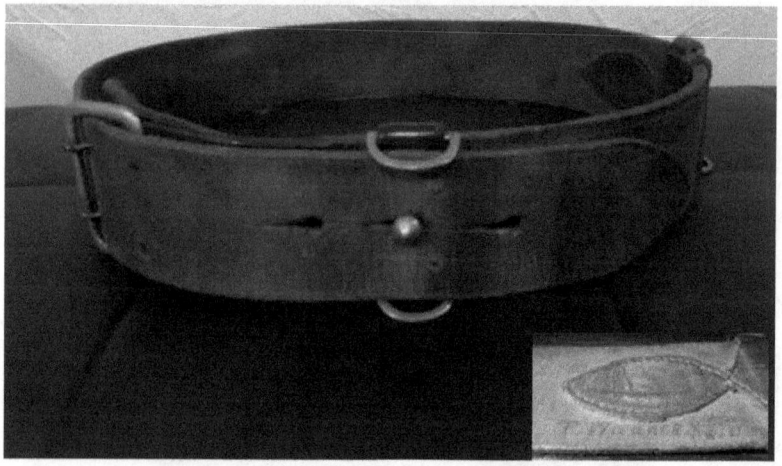

Tom's WW1 'Sam Browne' belt, with his name inscribed inside. Photo: Author

Gosport became the temporary home of the KRRC home base and training depot after a fire in December 1894 destroyed the main barracks at Winchester[53]. Known as 'The King's House' and designed by Sir Christopher Wren, the building was originally constructed for Charles II on the site of Winchester Castle. After the fire, it was rebuilt as two blocks to the original style and reopened in 1904[54]. Tom spent his first eight weeks at Gosport before transferring to Winchester at the end of March, 1904 after the new barracks were back in use.

Between 1902 and 1908, the 1st Battalion played its part in policing the British Empire by manning British Army garrisons in Malta, Crete and Egypt and Tom was stationed at all these locations. His postings are best recorded in a table, as they are taken from a variety of records.

Date	Age	Location
25/01/1904	19	Gosport
29/03/1904	19	Winchester
18/11/1904	20	HT Dunera
27/11/1904	20	Malta
27/02/1905	20	HT Dilwara
01/03/1905	20	Crete
25/02/1906	21	HT Dunera
01/03/1906	21	Cairo, Egypt
29/01/1909	24	HT Braemar Castle
12/02/1909	24	Gosport
09/11/1910	26	Alverstoke
29/09/1911	27	Aldershot
12/03/1912	27	Aldershot Isolation - Hospital (mumps) for 18 days
20/01/1913	27	Transferred to Army Reserve
05/08/1914	29	Winchester - Mobilised
12/08/1914	29	British Expeditionary Force - Rouen, Normandy

Postings between Recruitment and the British Expeditionary Force of 1914

After his initial training, Tom sailed for Malta on the HT Dunera, which was built in 1891, arriving on the 18th November 1904.

HT Dunera. Photo: Unknown

Malta was an important naval base for the British, and was a convenient stopping-off point for British soldiers during the Crimean War in the mid-nineteenth century. Roughly halfway between

Gibraltar and Port Said it was a useful stepping stone on the long haul between Britain and India. Although there were no major conflicts at the time, the British Fleet at Malta still needed protection and the average strength of the garrison around 1904 was 9,120 men. Malta was also home to military hospitals capable of treating hundreds of wounded personnel, and because of its strategic position in the Mediterranean was considered particularly important.

The KRRC contingent was stationed at the Floriana Barracks near the capital Valletta, well-positioned for defending the Grand Harbour.

Floriana Barracks Malta. Photo: Postcard Unknown

1903 brought a massive outbreak of 'Malta Fever' in the barracks, thought to be caused by the micrococcus melitensis bacterium[55]. Investigations found that the bacterium had been laying dormant in the soil and was disturbed during the building of the barracks. The KRRC had a higher incidence of the fever than the garrison as a whole, thought to be due to their arrival just after completion of a new block close to the Floriana building[56]. By 1904 there had been 320 hospital admissions and 12 deaths.

Tom was only in Malta for three months and managed to avoid infection. He embarked with the KRRC 1st Battalion on the Dilwara on the 27th February 1905 bound for Crete[57].

HT Dilwara. Photo: Unknown

Two days later, on the 1st March 1905, Tom arrived in Crete ready to help quell disturbances caused by the High Commissioner's refusal to consider union with Greece. The KRRC contingent consisted of some 400 men, but the British sector saw little of the revolt and only three reports of violence against the British were reported[58]. Tom was hospitalised with a high fever and shivering fits on the 3rd September 1905 and was treated there for ten days.

Insurgents continued to cause trouble until the end of 1905, but troops remained a few more weeks in order to uphold martial law. Tom was granted a Good Conduct Badge on the 21st January 1906 and left Crete for Cairo on the 25th February that year.

The Anglo-Egyptian War of 1882 left Britain with considerable influence over Egypt, as well as control over the Suez Canal[59]. In 1906, the German Empire began to support anti-British rule, and one of the British Army's objectives was to penetrate and close down the nationalist movements which sought to end British control. British troops continued their occupation until a treaty in 1922 gradually gave power back to the Egyptian government. The last British troops withdrew in 1954.

Tom was promoted to lance corporal on the 11th April 1906, soon after arriving in Egypt. On the 17th December 1907 he reverted to the rank of rifleman and forfeited his Good Conduct Badge as a result of misconduct. Nothing survives in Tom's records to suggest what he did to deserve the demotion, and the badge was restored one year later to the day.

The Braemar Castle, built in 1898 and one of the last ships of the Castle Line, departed Alexandria on the 30th January 1909 bound for Southampton[60]. On board was Tom with the 1st Battalion KRRC. They had been in Egypt for almost three years and completed a five year tour of overseas territories.

HT Braemar Castle. Photo: Unknown

Following his return to home duties at Gosport, Tom was re-appointed to the rank of lance corporal on the 29th October 1909. He must have been a crack shot with a rifle, because he and his team won the Excellent Challenge Cup for the 1st KRRC at the 1910 Portsmouth United Services Rifle Meeting[61]. Tom was moved to the Royal Marine Barracks at Alverstoke, about one mile west of Gosport, on the 9th November 1910 and on the 5th December 1910 he again forfeited his Good Conduct Badge. He was posted to Aldershot on the 29th September 1911 where the badge was restored. On the 12th March 1912, Tom was admitted to Aldershot Military Hospital for eighteen days suffering from mumps. He was promoted to corporal on the 11th June 1912, and in January 1913 after serving his nine years was discharged and transferred to the Reserve of Officers KRRC. He returned briefly to civilian life as an agricultural labourer and married in June of that year. His next military role would be as part of the British Expeditionary Force (BEF) in the First World War. Tom was mobilised at Winchester on the 5th August 1914. His first child, Freda Joy, would be born the following March. She would not see her father until she was four years old.

First World War

War was declared on Germany on Tuesday the 4th August 1914, and on Thursday the 13th August Tom embarked at Southampton with the 1st Battalion of the KRRC. They sailed across the English Channel to Le Havre and up the Seine to the port of Rouen in Normandy. Tom was part of the I Corps BEF, 2nd Division, 6th Infantry Brigade which also included the 2nd Battalion Oxford & Buckinghamshire Light Infantry and the 1st Battalion Royal Berkshire Regiment[62].

BATTLE	DATE
Battle of Mons	August 1914
First Battle of the Marne	September 1914
First Battle of the Aisne	September 1914
First Battle of Ypres	October 1914
Battle of Festubert	May 1915
Battle of Loos	September 1915
Battle of the Somme	Autumn 1916
Battle of Arras	November 1917
Battle of Cambrai	November 1917
Second Battle of the Somme	Autumn 1918
Battle of the Selle	October 1918

1st Battalion KRRC major battles in WW1

A week after arriving at Rouen, Tom had crossed the border between France and Belgium and by the 22nd August was preparing for his first enemy encounter. The Germans were pressing south in Belgium towards France and had reached the Mons canal. British infantry were positioned to the south of the canal with the intention of defending it from the German advance.

British Infantry waiting to advance in Mons. Photo: Unknown

Tom's brigade was located at Harmignes about 10km south east of Mons[63]. The British to the south successfully moved towards the canal, which was being prepared as an obstruction to the Germans by sinking barges and blowing up bridges.

The German assault on the canal came on Sunday the 23rd August. In spite of intense gunfire the canal was held until around midday, but soon after that the Germans crossed to the right of the British line. The French 5th Army had retreated, exposing the British right flank, and a withdrawal began, ending some two weeks later on the 5th September about 200 miles to the south of the River Marne near Paris.

The BEF suffered from lack of sleep and food shortages during the retreat, but soon recovered and launched an offensive to prevent the Germans advancing towards Paris. On the 9th September, Tom's brigade found that the bridges across the Marne at the centre of the BEF advance had not been demolished, and although there was a barricade across the middle of the bridge at Charly there were no opposing forces nearby. The barricade was dismantled, and the bridges to the east at Nogent and Azy were secured by the 1st and

4th Cavalry Brigades. By the end of the 9th September, the BEF occupied positions north of the river and with the German First and Second Armies withdrawing, the Battle of the Marne was over.

The 1st KRRC was not to rest long, as the BEF pushed northwards to the Aisne River to the east of Soissons. The Battle of the Aisne was to last from the 13th to the 15th September, and although the BEF succeeded in forcing the withdrawal of German troops across the river they counter-attacked on the 14th September and attempted to push back the 1st KRRC. After intense fighting, heavy losses were inflicted on the Germans and the position secured[64].

British Troops at Aisne September 1914. Photo: Robert Money[65]

What followed during the remainder of September and the first half of October became known as the 'Race to the Sea', as opposing sides tried to attack the other's northern position. Attention focused on Flanders, and by the second week of October the BEF arrived in northern France by train. The British believed that there was a break in the German lines around Ypres, and the First Battle of Ypres began on the 19th October 1914[66]. Tom was commissioned to 2nd lieutenant in the field that same month.

Ypres was a strategically important town in Flanders, with the high Mesen Ridge to the south and sited at the convergence of all the major roads in the area. The German offensive wanted to break through the allied lines to gain control of the English Channel ports. Fierce fighting took place with neither side gaining a distinct advantage, although the sheer number of German troops far outweighed the allies who were forced into a series of defensive manoeuvres. Of particular importance was the small village of Gheluvelt to the east of Ypres. This was the last remaining point in British hands which stood any chance of dominating the German line and represented a major crisis point in the battle.

On the morning of the 2nd November, German troops advanced towards the BEF line near the Menin Road to the east of Ypres.

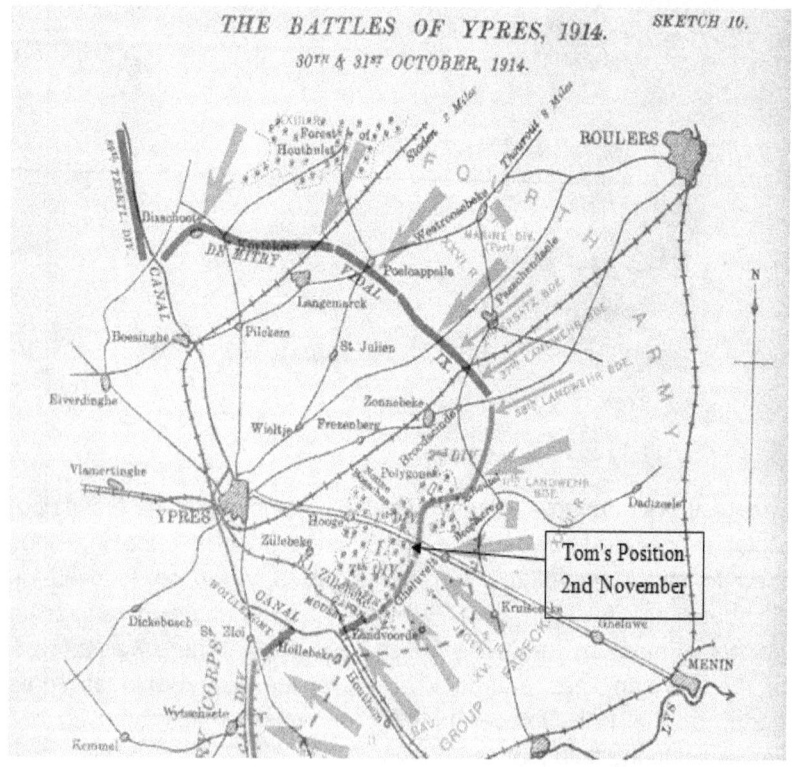

1st KRRC C Company Position 2nd November 1914, Sketch: Mitcham War Memorial [67]

The 1st KRRC C Company, which included Tom's platoon, together with the 1st Royal Berkshire and the 1st Coldstream had been commanded to leave the 2nd Division's line near Polygon Wood the day before and assist holding the line of the 7th Division to the south of the Menin road. Despite working through the night to improve their trench, when dawn broke, Tom's platoon discovered they had only a limited field of fire. The Germans managed to position machine guns in a house along the line of the trench. The gunners opened fire on the KRRC, who had no alternative but to lay low in their trenches. German troops quickly advanced into the trenches and C Company was overpowered. Nine officers and 437 men were killed or captured.

Tom sustained a gunshot wound to his arm and was taken prisoner along with other officers Captain W. P. Lynes, Captain H. E. Ward; Lieutenants A. M. Wakefield-Saunders, G. V. H. Gough; 2nd Lieutenants C. H. Reynard, C. F. Schoon, R. Richards and S. Lucas[68]

The precise events were not known to the commanding officer, because he was at headquarters based with the reserve A Company in adjoining woods and had no sight of the battle line. B, C and D Companies had been completely surrounded by the enemy, isolating them with no support. Over one thousand men were killed, wounded or missing and the 1st Battalion KRRC was reduced to the point where it practically ceased to exist.

All commissioned officers who were taken prisoner of war were required upon their release to write a report describing the circumstances of their capture. The reason might have been to reduce the possibility that an officer would voluntarily surrender, in the knowledge that he had a better chance of survival.

Tom wrote the following report after his return to England, although it is dated 2-11-1914, the day he was captured. It describes the events leading up to his capture, transcribed from his own handwriting.

STATEMENT regarding circumstances which led to capture:-

From October 23rd until November 2nd 1914 my Battalion was continually taking part in the very heavy fighting around Ypres.

During the night of the 1st November my Battalion was moved from part of the line held by the 2nd Div and went to the support of the part held by the 7th Div.

Arriving in the Woods near Hooge during the afternoon of the 1st Nov we rested a little until dark when we moved up into the Trenches on the Ypres Menin Road near Gheluvelt, these trenches were very badly situated running across a mangel wurzel field with no field of fire. The men of my Platoon improved the trench the best they could during the night.

Early on the morning of the 2nd Nov 1914 the Enemy started shelling my position very heavily and kept it up until about 2pm, when he was able to bring up some machine guns and occupy some Houses about 200 yds to my front.

These machine guns were able to fire right along my position and kept my men continuously in the bottom of the trench except a look out man every 40 yds.

The same time the Enemy attacked on the left flank and got into the trench almost immediately he made a frontal attack and my men were over powered.

During all his artillery fire he was known to be massing Infantry under a Wood(?) 200 yds in front of our position, this information was sent back to Headquarters but if it was ever received no one knows. We received no artillery support.

I was serving under orders of a Senior Officer during this time.

2-11-1914

Lieut T. Wadner

Kings Royal Rifle Corps

Name in full **Thomas Wadyer** Rank at time of Capture **2nd Lieut**
Date of Capture **1/11/1914** Place of Capture **Ypres Menin Road** near **Gheluvelt**
If wounded or otherwise **Gun shot wound left arm**
Company etc. **C** Unit **King's Royal Rifle Corps 6th** Brigade **2nd** Division
~~Whether Escaped or~~ Repatriated. Date of ~~Escape or~~ Repatriation **14/1/1919**
Date of arrival in England. **14-1-1919**
Present address **119 Gladstone Street Bedford**

(NOTE :— Refers to Unit, etc., in which serving at time of capture).

STATEMENT regarding circumstances which led to capture :—

From October 23rd until November 2nd, 1914 my Battalion was continually taking part in the very heavy fighting around Ypres

During the night of the 1st Nov my Battalion was moved from part of the line held by the 2nd Div and went to the support of the part held by the 7th Div

Arriving in the Woods near Hooge during the afternoon of the 1st Nov we rested a little until dusk when we moved up into the Trenches on the Ypres Menin Road near Gheluvelt, these trenches were very badly situated running across a mangel Wurzel field with no field of fire. The men of my Platoon improved the trench the best they could during the night

Early on the morning of the 2nd Nov, 1914 the Enemy started shelling my position very heavily and kept it up until about 2 pm, when he was able to bring up some mach. guns and occupy some Houses about 300 yds to my front. These machine guns were able to fire right along my position and kept my men ~~continuously~~ continually in the bottom of the trench except a look out man every 40 yds,

The same time the Enemy attacked on the left flank and got into the trench almost immediately — he made a Frontal attack and my men were over powered

To
The Secretary, War Office,
Whitehall, London, S.W.1.

P.T.O

Circumstances of capture report hand-written by Tom (1). Image: The National Archives[69] (OGL)

During all his Artillery fire he was known to be massing Infantry under a *x yds* 200 yds in front of our position. this information was sent back to Headquarters but if it ever arrived no one knows. We received no Artillery support

I was serving under a *other of* Senior Officer during this time. 9-11-1914

Lieut T. Wadner
Kings Royal Rifle Corps

Circumstances of capture report hand-written by Tom (2). Image: The National Archives[70] (OGL)

Volume 5 of The Annals of the KRRC[71] provides a broader perspective of what happened on the 2nd November 1914, and the following is taken directly from there, including the account from the official history:

November 2 was much the same kind of day as November 1, in that the Germans and French both attacked, leaving the situation pretty well unchanged at the end of the day; but it is an eventful day in our annals, as our 1st Battalion had three companies surrounded and annihilated.

The following account of the disaster is taken from the 'Official History':

'Bernard's detachment of the French IX Corps - increased from eight battalions to ten, with four groups of artillery, and placed under General Vidal - was to attack south-eastward towards Becelaere, as on the previous day, but this village was strongly occupied, so, on Sir D. Haig's suggestion, the objective was changed. Pursuing the idea of a north to south counter-attack, Vidal arranged to pass through the left of the 1st Division between the Menin Road and Polygon Wood, and to attack south-eastwards against the curve in the German line near Gheluvelt. This was practically to follow the route of the Worcestershire on October 31. In co-operation with this movement of General Vidal, the British 1st Division was to attack eastwards, so that the enemy would be caught between two fires.

The infantry advance/should have taken place at 10 a.m., and the artillery preparation began in good time; but, owing to various causes - the confusion due to the mixture of French and British troops, and the former being new to the ground - it was not till after 12 noon that Vidal's battalions began to approach the British line; but here, as near Wytschaete [on 01 Nov, the previous day], the enemy took the initiative.

'To avoid interference with Vidal's advance, the artillery of the 1st Division had received instructions not to fire from 10.30 a.m. onwards on the ground near the Menin Road, which could not be overlooked by ground observers. This, unfortunately, gave the enemy a great opportunity. From 8.30 a.m. onwards his 30th Division, with the XXVII

Reserve Corps north of it, had shown a disposition to push forward on either side of the Menin Road, where stood D Company of the 1st Royal Berkshire, three companies of the 1st K.R.R.C., and the 1st Coldstream, the last being under the establishment of a company in men and having only two officers. One company of the K.R.R.C. and two of the Berkshire were in support. These troops, it will be recalled, had only taken over from the 3rd Brigade after dark, less than twelve hours earlier, and had found but shallow disconnected lengths of trench, barely marking a front, without any wire or, of course, any dug-outs. Across the road [the Menin Road], where the 200 Coldstream stood, was a barricade. Behind this was a group of houses and a farm building which had not been prepared for defence; for, though the men in this sector worked hard during the night, they were too tired to effect much. When daylight came and they were thoroughly worn out, it was found that the field of fire, owing to a ridge on our side and a falling slope on the other, was limited to from 50 to 150 yards. This would have been sufficient if there had been a good obstacle in front of the trenches, and if the supporting artillery had had direct observation on the narrow field of fire. It was inadequate in the circumstances, particularly as hedges obstructed view along the line and interfered with mutual support. To make matters worse, less than 100 yards in front of the British line, bordering on the road, was a small house, to burn which all endeavours had been in vain.

'The barricade on the road was early blown away, and one machine gun of the K.R.R.C., which covered it, put out of action. Though held off elsewhere, the Germans managed to get up a machine gun into the small house about 9.30 a.m. Another party with another machine gun worked its way through a gap of over 60 yards between the Berkshire Company and the K.R.R.C. north of it, and now opened fire at a hundred yards range into the backs of the Rifles. This battalion had definite orders not to retire, and, with the Berkshire and the Coldstream, still kept off all attackers. Invaluable aid was rendered by the artillery, particularly by two guns of the 116th Battery, a couple of hundred yards behind the line.

About 11 a.m., soon after the British batteries had, according to orders, ceased to fire on the area near the Menin Road, the Germans of the 30th Division, under the covering fire of the machine gun in the small house, came on boldly down the road in parties of thirty and forty, followed on either side of it by others crawling in twos and threes. Getting up close to the British trenches they overpowered the Coldstream, taking prisoner Captain E. G. Christie-Miller, who was in command, and capturing or killing nearly one-half of their scanty number. They then turned against the three companies of the K.R.R.C., already attacked in front, machine-gunned from the rear, and bombed by parties working up the trench from their right. Then came a final rush. There was a melee between the Germans and the two left companies, but it lasted only a few minutes. The right company held out a little longer, but in the end 9 officers and 437 men of the Battalion were killed or captured.'

The officers missing, all of whom were prisoners of war, were: Captain W. P. Lynes, Captain H. E. Ward (3rd Buffs); Lieutenants A. M. Wakefield-Saunders, G. V. H. Gough; 2nd Lieutenants C. H. Reynard, C. F. Schoon, R. Richards, S. Lucas, and T. Wadner.

Prisoner of War

After Tom was captured, he and his fellow officers were marched behind the German line to one of the Fourth Army control posts. There they would have been questioned to obtain information about the positions and strengths of the Allies, although it is unthinkable that anything was given away.

Being November, darkness fell quite early so it was unlikely that the prisoners were moved on before the following day. They probably spent a difficult night under armed guard, but hopefully Tom would have been treated for the gunshot wound to his arm. On the 3rd November, Tom and the others set off to a destination unknown to them. They arrived at Crefeld Prisoner Of War camp on the 5th November.

Crefeld is about 200 miles from Ypres. It sits on the Rhine about 12 miles northwest of Dusseldorf and about 50 miles from the Belgian border to the west. Although using today's E17 route the journey would have taken just over three hours by car, a military truck back in 1914 would have been slower and no doubt there would have been frequent stops.

Had he not been an officer, Tom would have been detained in a wooden hut holding up to 250 prisoners. Bedding would have been basic, probably straw mattresses, and furniture sparse. The camp would have been secured by high barbed wire fencing and carefully guarded. Crefield was one of the earliest on record where officers were held in camps reserved especially for them[72]. These camps were less austere, and often located in existing buildings such as hotels or barracks. The captives were not required to perform labouring tasks, and generally suffered more from boredom than anything else.

In 1915, Crefield held 133 British officers and 21 orderlies, as well as nearly 300 other nationalities[73]. The camp was situated on the outskirts of the city which had a population of around 125,000. Conditions were reported to have been excellent and there were few complaints about the health and well-being of the prisoners[74]. Promotions that were a result of time in service continued to be made to prisoners of war, and Tom was promoted to lieutenant in May 1915.

Crefeld POW Buildings 1915. Photo: Unknown[75]

Taken to Crefeld along with Tom were the other officers captured at Gheluvelt on the 2nd November. They are all included on a Crefeld record sheet dated the 5th November 1914. Captain Lynes died at the age of 43 on the 14th October 1916 in captivity, and must have been repatriated at that time because he is buried in St Mary's Churchyard, Barnsley, Gloucestershire.

A German record sheet from the Officer's Camp at Crefeld shows the place and date of Tom's capture, his injury and a few other personal details.

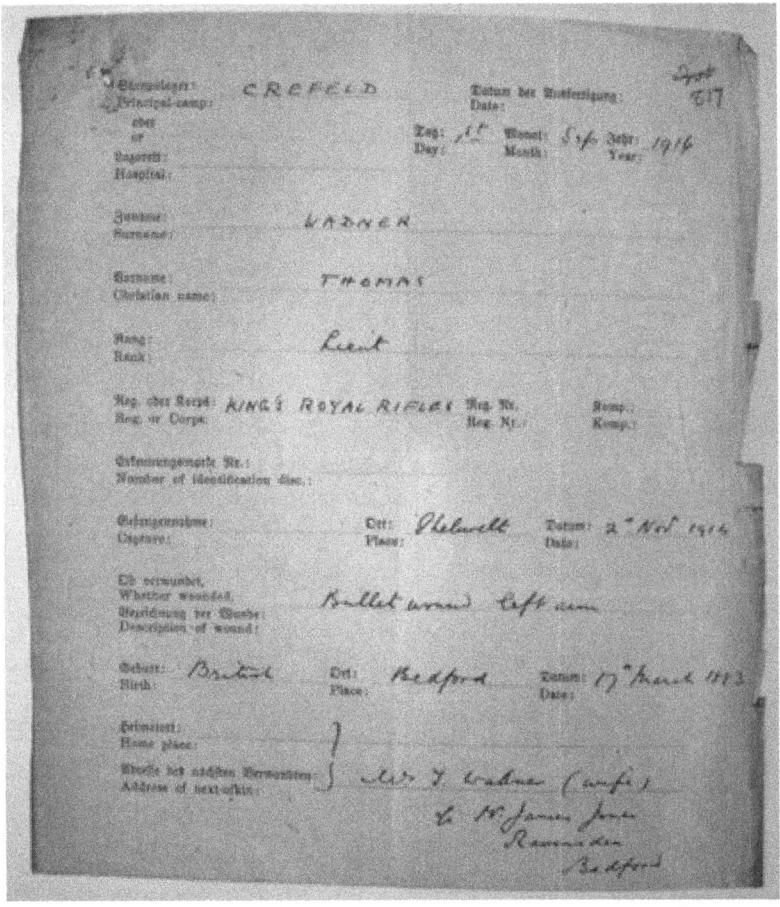

Record from Crefeld POW Camp September 1916. Image: The National Archives[76] (OGL)

Tom gave his year of birth as 1883 when he was captured. This would have made him appear two years older than he was; thirty two instead of thirty years of age. Prisoners were required to give only their name, rank and date of birth when captured, so perhaps giving an incorrect age was a simple act of defiance.

The Crefeld record is dated September 1916, but there is no clue regarding why it was filled out at that time. It is surprising that Tom's army file should contain a German document, so it is possible that it was produced to send back to England as a matter of record, perhaps to 'twist the knife'.

Just over four months after Tom was sent to Crefeld, an announcement in the Bedfordshire Times and Independent reported that his first daughter Freda Joy was born at Ravensden on the 4th March 1915.

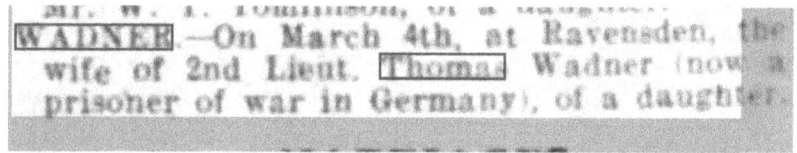

Classified Section from The Bedfordshire Times and Independent 4th March 1915

Tom was made up to captain through a time in service promotion on the 1st January, 1917. Towards the end of that year, the camp at Crefeld had become hopelessly overcrowded, and on the 30th November Tom was moved to Freiburg, close to the French and Swiss borders. Clearly out to confuse the enemy, he again gave an incorrect birth year, this time of 1884.

The officer's prisoner of war camp at Freiburg was located in the old university building in the centre of the town. The French border was only about 13 miles away, and airborne raids on the town began in 1914. Many civilians were killed and buildings destroyed[77], and locating the camp there was an attempt to stop the attacks.

Freiburg also suffered severe overcrowding and on the 11th December 1917, six weeks after he arrived, Tom was moved about 300 miles north to Holzminden, not far from Hanover. Holzminden had opened a couple of months prior to his arrival, and mostly housed officers of which there were about 550. Approximately 100 lower ranks were imprisoned there, and these acted as servants to the officers[78].

The prisoners occupied two four-storey buildings, known as Block A and Block B. Kitchens, a post room, bath house and other services were housed in a series of separate wooden buildings. There is no year given for the photograph below, and no record of whether Tom was in Block A or B. However, there is a fair chance that he is in the picture but its resolution is insufficient to pick out individual faces, especially those further away at the windows.

Prisoners and Guards at Block B, Holzminden. Photo: Wikipedia Commons

Holzminden has two polarised reputations. First, it was run under a harsh set of rules, although the officers probably fared better than the lower ranking orderlies. Their diet was poor, caused mainly by sanctions placed upon Germany which meant that food was scarce, even for the general population. On the brighter side, the officers were allowed to receive parcels from home and these often contained favourite foods.

The second reputation is for the escape of twenty-nine prisoners on the night of the 24th July 1918. Taking some nine months to excavate, a tunnel was created between an entrance underneath a staircase in Block B and the perimeter fence. The plan was for eighty-six to escape, but the thirtieth man got stuck in the tunnel. Nevertheless, the camp holds the record for the number of prisoners to escape in one attempt. Tom might well have been involved in the excavation of the tunnel, although he had been moved before the actual escape attempt.

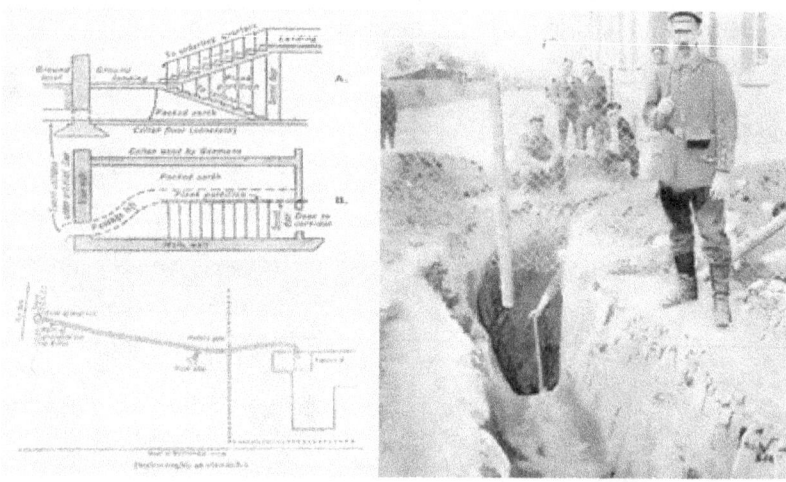

Holzminden Tunnel Entrance, Route, and After Discovery [79]. Photo: Unknown

Towards the end of 1917 the Dutch government mediated an agreement whereby British and German officers who had been in captivity for more than three years could be interned in Holland and Switzerland, both neutral countries.

Tom is listed as 'Interned Military' on the 24th February, 1918 in what appears to be a Dutch document. Unfortunately, no location is given. There were a total of the following interned: 33,105 Belgians (among which were 406 officers), 1751 British (139 officers), 1461 Germans (68 officers), 8 French (5 officers) and 4 American officers. The interns from France and America were from damaged aircraft that landed on Dutch soil[80].

The main internment camp was at Groningen, although this was mainly used for military personnel who entered the country to escape enemy hands. For instance, around 1500 reservists from the Royal Navy were forced to enter Holland to escape capture by the Germans, and by international law they had to be interned for the rest of the war.

It is unlikely that Tom would have been held at Groningen because he was a very long-term prisoner holding the rank of captain. He would probably have been interned at a hotel or boarding house, or perhaps billeted in a family home. These less austere conditions were located mostly on the outskirts of The Hague and Scheveningen. Tom would have had to sign a document whereby he gave his word of honour not to escape. He kept his word.

Repatriation

Tom sailed home from Holland via Rotterdam to Hull on the P&O Liner SS Khyber, leaving on the 13th January 1919. The ship hit a sandbank off the North Norfolk coast and had to be refloated on the rising tide during the morning of the 14th[81]. Tom was eventually repatriated at Ripon, not far inland from Hull, on the 15th January 1919 and immediately given two months leave.

SS Khyber. Photo: Simplon - The Passenger Ship Website[82]

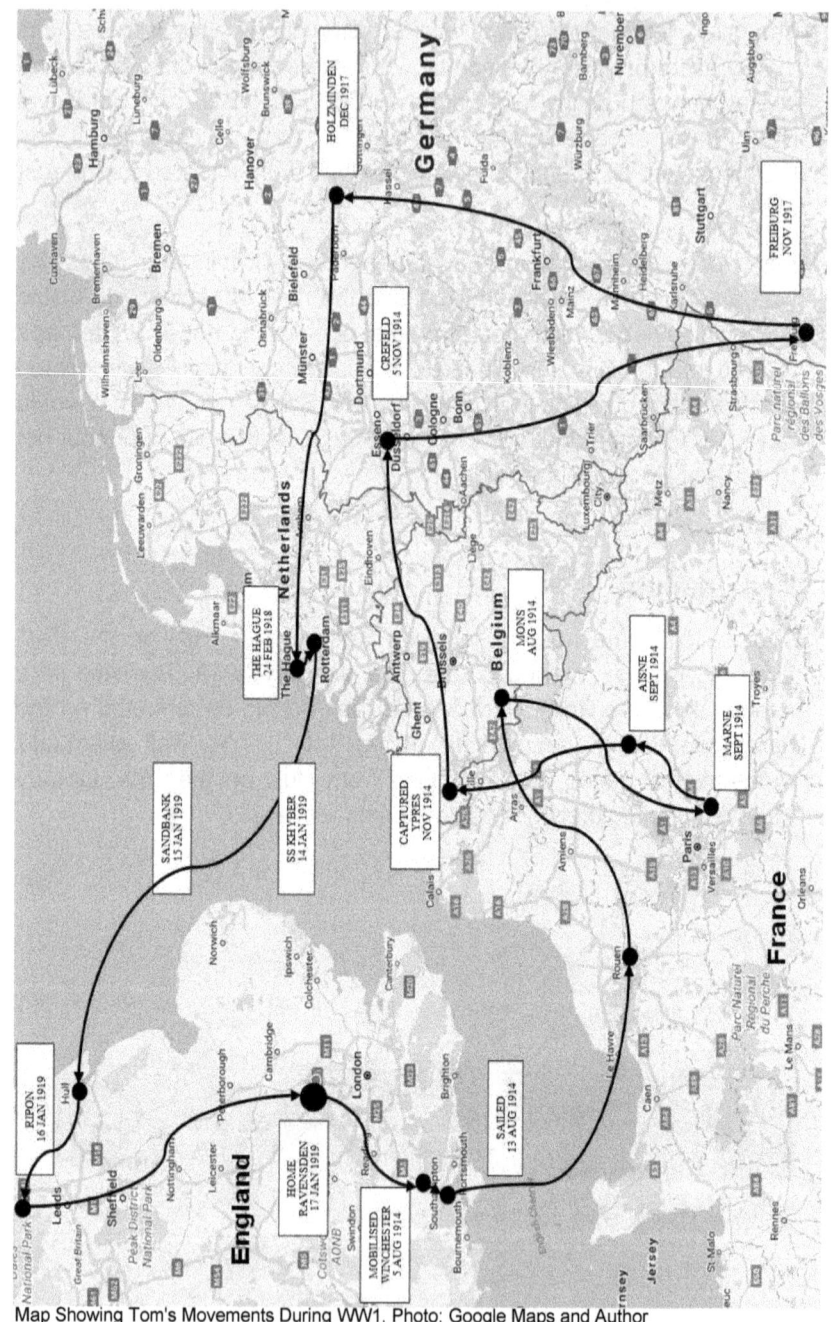
Map Showing Tom's Movements During WW1. Photo: Google Maps and Author

Every returning officer and man was given a copy of a hand-written message from King George V, which read:

The Queen joins me in welcoming you on your release from the miseries & hardships, which you have endured with so much patience and courage.

During these many months of trial, the early rescue of our gallant Officers & Men from the cruelties of their captivity has been uppermost in our thoughts.

We are thankful that this longed for day has arrived, & that back in the old Country you will be able once more to enjoy the happiness of a home & to see good days among those who anxiously look for your return.

George R.I.

Upon his return from leave in the middle of March 1919 Tom was posted to Egypt on "Drafting Conducting Duty". Following that, on the 5th August 1919 he was ordered to join the 5th Battalion KRRC (Light Reserve Brigade) at Rugeley Camp near Cannock Chase, Staffordshire. This was largely a training camp, providing instruction in musketry, scouting, signalling, physical training, gas warfare and many other skill areas. Tom was given further orders to proceed to India on the 14th September 1919. However, after fifteen years in the army, four of which spent as a prisoner of war, Tom had other ideas. He resigned his commission on the 16th August 1919 citing 'civilian business and family difficulties' as his reasons.

It isn't clear to what 'civilian business' Tom was referring, but his second child, Betty, was due to be born in December 1919. That was most likely high on his list of priorities, and he wanted a fresh start for his wife and first child who were living with his mother and step father in Ravensden.

Even though his request to resign was approved, the army was not going to be completely over and done with. Tom was recalled from the Reserve of Officers for an emergency between the 16th April and the 5th June 1921, and his retirement pay was suspended between those dates. The dates coincide with two major events in history.

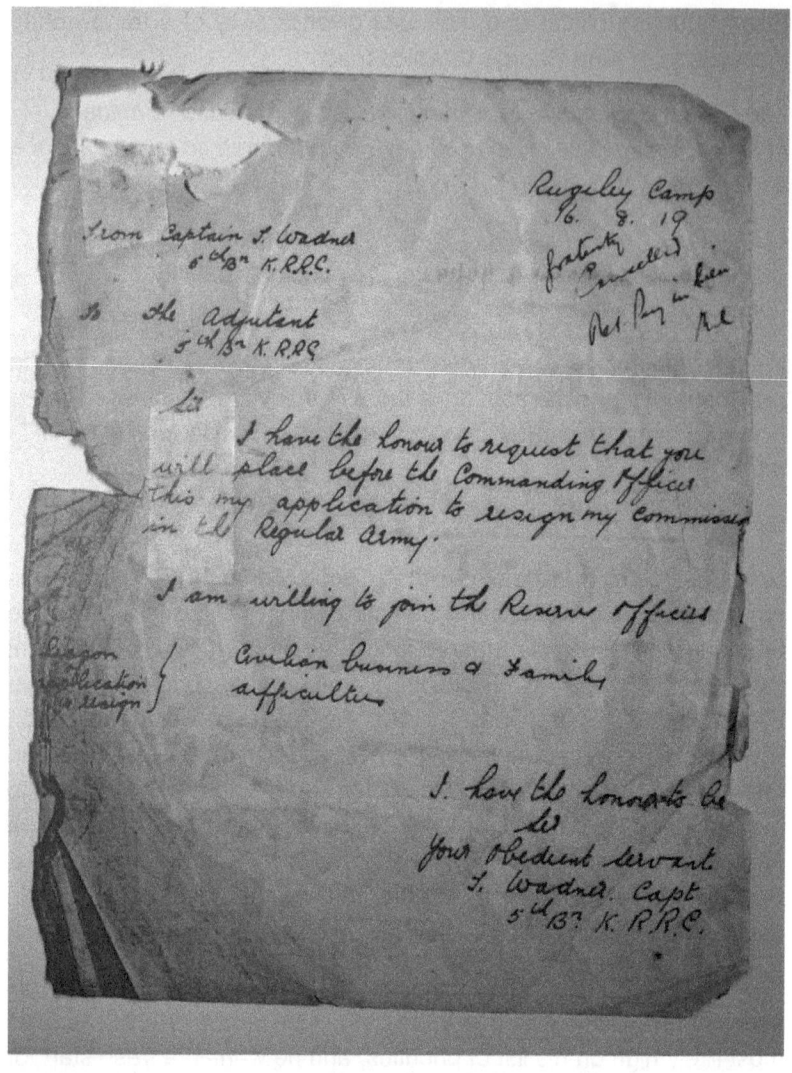

Letter Resigning Commission. Image: The National Archives[83] (OGL)

First there was the miner's strike, called after mine owners demanded cuts in wages and longer working hours. The mines were returned to private control on the 31st March 1921, after being nationalised during the First World War. The miners asked for support from rail and transport workers, and a strike by these three powerful unions was to begin on the 15th April. The 'triple alliance' fell apart, and although the miners continued with their action they were eventually forced back to work.

The second possibility was the Irish War of Independence. The Irish Republican Army and British security forces were in armed conflict between 1919 and 1921. On the 3rd May 1921, the Province of Northern Ireland was created by the UK government and elections were held on the 24th May. By the summer of that year, there would be around 50,000 British soldiers in Ireland.

War Medals

Tom received three medals for the part he played during the war. These were (left to right in the photograph) the 1914 Star, the British War Medal and the Victory Medal.

Tom's Medals. Photos: Courtesy of Clinton Blackburn

The 1914 Star was awarded to officers and men who served in Belgium between the 5th August and the 22nd November 1914. It recognises their contribution in holding back the German army during the opening weeks of the war, and their participation in the battles of Mons, the retreat to the Seine, Le Cateau, the Marne, the Aisne and the first battle of Ypres.

The British War Medal, 1914-18, was awarded to officers and men serving in conflict at any time during the war. Struck in silver with the head of King George on the front and St. George on horseback on the reverse, the rim is inscribed with Tom's service number, rank, name and unit.

The Allied Victory Medal was awarded to officers and men who received the 1914 Star. Struck in bronze, the medal shows the classical figure of 'Victoria' holding a palm branch on the front, and on the back is inscribed 'THE GREAT WAR FOR CIVILISATION 1914-1919'. The rim is inscribed with Tom's service number, rank, name and unit.

Tom's Medal Card. Image: The National Archives[84] (OGL)

Tom's medal card shows the applications made for his three medals. According to the card, he also received the 'clasp and roses'. This turned the 1914 Star into a 'Mons Star', and was awarded to those who had operated within range of enemy mobile artillery during the 1914 Star qualifying period.

Ceremonial Sword

Tom somehow gained possession of a sword and scabbard, which he brought home when he was repatriated.

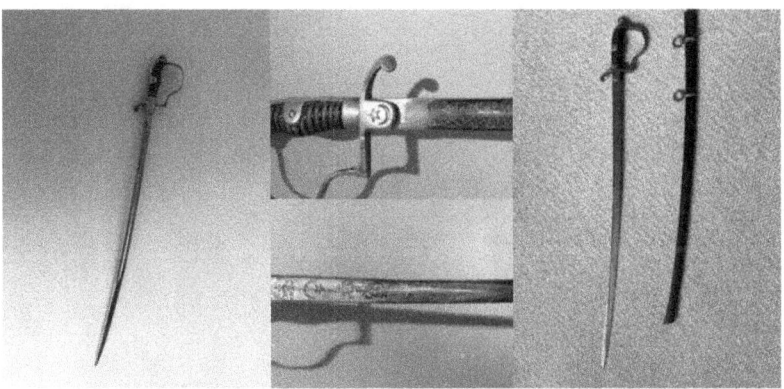

Ceremonial Sword. Photos: Courtesy of Clinton Blackburn

The crescent and star is a good indication that the sword is either Turkish or maybe German, given the Ottoman Empire/Germany alliance at the start of WW1. From the elaborate decoration on the blade, it is more likely to be a dress or ceremonial sword than one used in anger.

How Tom came by the sword is a matter of conjecture. Not only was he imprisoned for most of WW1, the KRRC played no part in Gallipoli in 1915. Nor could he have been involved in the occupation of Constantinople when British, French and Italian forces occupied the city in 1918.

Tom was moved from Holzminden POW camp to internment in The Hague at the beginning of 1918, and it is possible that it was there that he came by the sword. British officers who took part in the Gallipoli campaign might have picked up an enemy sword, or Tom might even have acquired it from a German officer. The officers were mostly housed in boarding houses and hotels so probably mixed together to some extent.

However the sword was obtained, it took pride of place in all of Tom's houses after he returned to England.

Tom's Siblings

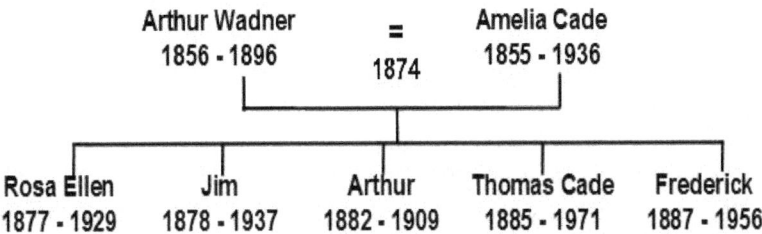

To help put Tom's life in context, the following pages draw a thumbnail sketch of what happened to each of his siblings.

Following the tragic death of their father in 1896 and the marriage of their mother to Jimmy Jones in 1900, it was not only Tom who found himself without a home at the beginning of a new century. Each of his brothers and sister have their own tale to tell.

Rosa Ellen had left home when the family moved to Goldington Highfields in 1891, perhaps because the cottage was smaller than the one they lived in at Mount Pleasant but more likely because she would have left school at that time and needed to find work.

Jim had continued in agricultural labouring so he could contribute to the family income, but when the family broke up he took a room in Kempston and changed his occupation to brewery work.

Arthur, being disabled, might have been the one sibling who Amelia took with her when she remarried, but he left for a new life in Leighton Buzzard. He rented a room and learned the trade of basket making.

Fred was the youngest at thirteen. He went to stay with Rosa and earned money as a grocery delivery boy.

Rosa Ellen

Rosa Ellen's birth certificate clearly states her name as Rose, but apart from that one record, she is referred to as Rosa. Perhaps Amelia and Arthur changed their mind about her name shortly after she was born, or maybe the registrar made a mistake recording the birth.

At the age of fourteen in 1891, Rosa was working as a servant for a schoolmaster and his family at 2 Duke Street in Bedford. The house is about fifty yards from the junction of Duke Street with Mill Street and still stands today, although it is now used as a business premises.

2 Duke Street, Bedford. Photo: Google Streetview

Since Rosa had left home before her mother re-married, she did not suffer the indignity of being told there was no room for her in Jimmy Jones' family home. She married Walter Stephen Odell, a railway coach cleaner from Cranfield, at Goldington Parish Church on the 25th December 1889. A Christmas Day wedding sounds very romantic, but in the nineteenth century it was often the only day when working class couples could guarantee that they would both be allowed off work. Witnesses are recorded as Rosa's brother Jim, and Mary Burrage, although the second witness could have been Jim's wife-to-be Mary Surridge.

Rosa was twenty three, two years older than Walter, when they married. They had a son, Walter James, one year later in December 1900. He was the first of ten children born over the following twenty years, the last one, Florence, arriving in 1919. There was a regularity to the births, one every two years, except for Emma who arrived a year earlier than usual in 1909. Then there was a break of four years, which Rosa made up for by having twins Enos and Francis on the 4th October 1913.

In 1901, Rosa and Walter lived at 63 Thompson Street, New Bradwell, now part of Milton Keynes. The street is not listed in the 1881 census, so the houses will have been fairly new in 1901.

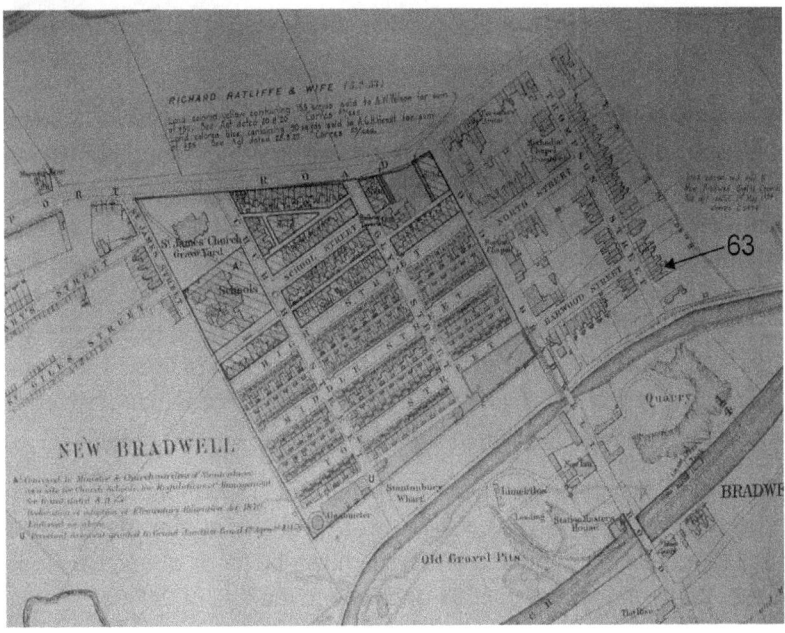

New Bradwell Street Map 1891 (Extract, Thompson Street top right). Photo: MK Heritage[85]

Originally the road continued until it met the River Great Ouse, but the last house in Thompson Street is now number 55. The final fifty yards or so of the street was demolished to make way for a new housing development in Bridgeway. The last house shown in the photograph below is number 55, and it is likely that Rosa's house, which would have been four along to the right from this one, was of a similar style.

Thompson Street, Bradwell. Photo: Google Streetview

The family moved a mile or so south to Well Yard, Bradwell Abbey, Old Bradwell in about 1910 and it is there that their daughter Emma was born. Well Yard included about half a dozen dwellings and was situated in the proximity of the Victoria Inn, Manor Farm and St Lawrence's Church, although the latter is the only recognisable present day structure following extensive redevelopment. In 1913, the family moved to 34 Vicarage Road, a stone's throw from St. Lawrence's Church. That is where Rosa gave birth to twins Enos and Francis, and the family was still living there when their last child Florence Amy was born when Rosa was forty two years old.

Rosa died from stomach cancer on the 8th September 1929 when she was aged fifty two. Walter was present at her death, and registered it using the name she was known by for all of her life, Rosa Ellen. Walter remarried in 1931 and lived to the age of 94.

Jim

Jim continued to work as a farm labourer on Jackman's Farm in Goldington after his father Arthur's death. On the 10th August 1900 he apprehended two tramps who had stolen potatoes and pieces of iron from the farm, and chased them for some three hundred yards. Jim gave evidence at Bedford Division Police Court on Saturday the 18th August and the offenders were remanded, but they had no fixed address and were never charged[86].

After leaving the family home later that year, Jim found lodgings at 17 Howard Street, Kempston and at the age of twenty three was working as a malster. He would have been responsible for preparing barley by soaking it in water, turning it regularly for a few days until it began to germinate and then roasting the grain to produce the malt needed for brewing beer. Jim could have been working for local brewer Thomas Jarvis who also owned The Wellington public house not far from Howard Street on Bedford Road, or perhaps for rival Bedford brewer Charles Wells.

Jim married Mary Ann Surridge from Bletsoe on the 1st July 1901 at Bletsoe Parish Church. Witnesses at the wedding were Fanny Surridge, Mary's older sister, and John Castleman. John was from Thurleigh and was born about the same time as Jim, so was probably an old friend.

At the time of her marriage, Mary was a cook for a military family at 61 DeParys Avenue in Bedford, now Elcombe House Care Home. The Hudsons were a large family who also employed a parlour maid and housemaid. Head of the family was Lieutenant Colonel William Hudson, a Knight Commander of the Indian Empire. With his wife, three daughters and three sons between the ages of twelve and twenty five, Mary would have had a great deal of cooking on her hands.

The couple's first home was at 1H Beaconsfield Street in Bedford, and it is there that their first child Lily Ivy was born on the 14th January 1902. That house is a traditional two up two down, so although Lily's birth certificate clearly shows number 1H in two places,

Jim was more likely telling the registrar it was number 'one eight'. Lily was followed by May in 1906, Arthur John in 1908 and William James in 1912.

In 1906 Jim and Mary lived in Bromham at Clapham End, and in the 1911 census Jim's occupation is recorded as 'Groom on farm'. The family occupied a farm cottage at Vicarage Green on Oakley Road. It is interesting that although Jim is given the title of head of the household on the census form, it is Mary who filled out the form and signed it. In 1891 at the age of thirteen, Jim was already working as an agricultural labourer so although he had attended school in Thurleigh and then Clapham Parochial, he must have dropped out at least a year early and maybe wasn't the most legible of writers.

Around 1912, the family moved to 9 London Row, Clapham. London Row was a terrace of thirteen cottages on Clapham High Street, built in 1892, about 200 metres from Highbury Grove in the Clapham Folly direction. Daughter Lily attended Queens Park Board School in 1912, and May and Arthur were admitted to Clapham Parochial School on the 21st October 1912 (the school was rebuilt in the 1960s as the Ursula Taylor). May stayed at the school until the 30th July 1920 when she reached fourteen years of age. The record shows she had been vaccinated against measles and whooping cough. Arthur left on the 21st December 1922 to start work, the records showing he had missed out on the whooping cough jab but had been given the one for measles.

There are no WW1 military records for Jim. This could be because he worked for the Bedford District Gas Company between 1914 and 1937, and probably first joined what was the Kempston Gas Company in Mill Lane, next to the River Ouse. In 1924, this was incorporated with the Bedford Gaslight Company to become Bedford District Gas[87]. The supply of gas was essential to keep the iron and steel industry running, and anything that provided ammunition and equipment for the war effort was deemed a scheduled occupation. This makes it likely that Jim would have been exempted from military service and issued a certificate by the recruiting authorities and a badge to show that he was engaged on war service.

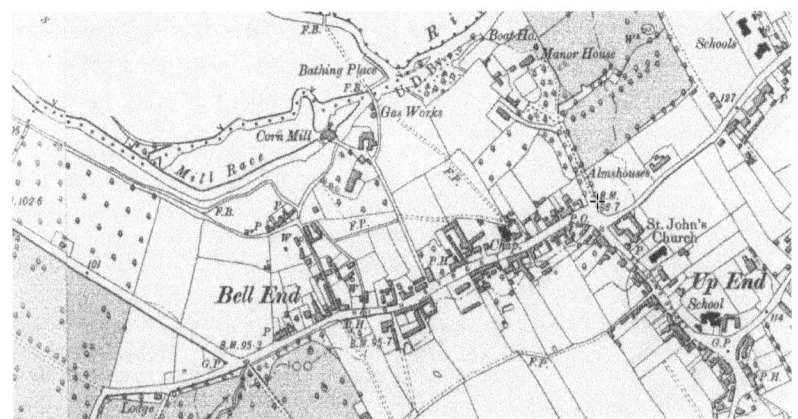

Kempston Gas Company, Mill Lane, 1913. Map: National Library of Scotland

Shortly before Christmas 1919, Jim had a lucky escape. He was a key witness at the inquest of the death of John Harold Johnson, aged thirty eight, who was struck by a falling lamp post. Jim was cycling along St. Mary's, Bedford and planned to turn right into Cauldwell Street. He had to change his mind because his progress was blocked by a lorry travelling in the opposite direction. The lorry behind him hit the rear of his bicycle and pushed him forwards a few yards, wrecking his back wheel. The lorry skidded, shed its load and hit the lamp post, which fell onto the luckless Mr. Johnson. The driver claimed that Jim had caused him to brake suddenly, resulting in the fatal accident. The Coroner, though, found that the accident was due to a greasy road which had caused the braking lorry to skid, hit Jim's bicycle and knock down the lamp post[88]. The verdict was one of accidental death.

Around 1928, London Row in Clapham was renamed The Terrace and the electoral register shows the family living at number nine in 1929. They moved to a newly built house at 12 Council Houses, a stone's throw from their home of nearly twenty years.

Tragedy struck three days before Christmas in 1930, when Jim and Mary's son Arthur died suddenly at the age of twenty two. He had pulmonary tuberculosis and suffered a massive bleed from his lungs.

Jim's new house was the last of twelve constructed by Bedford Rural District Council on the old Clapham recreation ground, with a cinder track leading to them from Highbury Grove. The road is now made up, and known as The Close. The houses, with their massive gardens, are still there but more have been built between them and the houses re-numbered.

12 Council Houses, Clapham (left). Photo: Google Streetview

Jim died on the 6th December 1937 at the age of fifty nine after contracting pulmonary tuberculosis, a drawn-out illness which had begun two years earlier. His son William, who by then had left home and lived just around the corner at 31 Highbury Grove, was present at the death.

Tom, together with many family members, attended his brother's funeral which took place on Friday the 10th December 1937 at Clapham Parish Church. His wreath was inscribed 'With deepest sympathy, Tom and Violet'.

Mary continued to live in the same house with daughters Lily and May until her death in 1953.

Arthur

With Arthur suffering a disability, he might have tried to find some way to stay with his mother after she remarried, but instead he moved to a boarding house at 33 Lake Street, Leighton Buzzard. In 1901, Arthur and the other boarder at the house, William Tanney, were working as basket makers. This is surprising, given his family background of agricultural labouring over many generations, but his disability might have been sufficiently severe to prevent him from working on the land. Basket making, as well as straw plaiting for hats, had been a traditional cottage industry for the town since 1750 and Lake Street was well known as the centre[89]. The River Ouzel, which runs through the town, provided a particularly rich source of willow from the osier beds planted for the purpose.

Lake Street has been extensively redeveloped since Arthur boarded there. The last property on the 'odd' side of the street is a shop at number 51, until the numbers re-appear after a petrol station on a major roundabout beginning at the town library. Number 33 has disappeared, but was probably around the location of the car park for Leighton Buzzard FC.

Arthur didn't stay long in Leighton Buzzard. On the 17th September 1903 he travelled to Liverpool, where he boarded the SS Ionian together with 946 other passengers bound for a new life in Canada. His destination is given variously as Quebec, Montreal and Toronto and the trip by steamer would have taken about seven days.

SS Ionian. Photo: Norway Heritage[90]

The steamship was built in Belfast in 1901 and launched in September that year, so was almost new. It was 470 feet long and 58 feet wide, which doesn't seem particularly large considering the number of passengers it could carry. There was accommodation for about 130 first class passengers, 160 second class, and another 800 travelling third class[91]. Arthur would not have been able to afford anything other than third class, but since the ship was not filled to capacity with only 947 on board, his voyage might have been a little more comfortable than he expected.

In 1914 at the start of the First World War, and after thirteen years of carrying emigrants to Canada, all of the SS Ionian's first class passenger facilities were removed, and she was converted to a troop carrier travelling to Bombay via Suez. She was never destined for a long life and was sunk on the 20th October 1917 by a mine, two miles off the Pembrokeshire coast en route from Milford Haven to Plymouth. The mine was laid by German submarine UC-51. Seven people lost their lives[92].

One of Tom's military records mentions his older brother Arthur in a list of his next of kin in 1904, as does his brother Fred's. Tom's is annotated 'Address not known', but Fred's has it as 37 Dundas Street, Toronto, Canada. Either Tom simply didn't remember, or Arthur had only kept in touch with his other brother.

Dundas Street is in the town of Oakville in the Halton Region, part of the Greater Toronto area. Early in the nineteenth century, British immigrants began settling there, and although Oakville would seem to be a random choice of destination, basket making was becoming a major industry in the town. It looks as though Arthur knew exactly what he was planning to do when he bought his ticket.

Most residents in the Dundas Street district were working class people of British or Irish descent, and much of the housing was substandard[93]. Overcrowding and the lack of basic hygiene facilities were major problems, which resulted in the rapid spread of disease.

Dundas Street, Toronto, c1910. Photos: City of Toronto Archives[94]

Tuberculosis was raging across Canada in the late 1800s and by 1890 it was the cause of about 20% of all deaths. Special hospitals had to be set up to deal with the massive number of cases, and to try to contain what was an aggressively contagious disease with a 45% mortality rate.

The most important action taken was to separate the sufferers from the community at large. The first Canadian sanatorium was the Muskoka Cottage Hospital. It opened in 1898 and patients had to pay to be treated. Four years later, the Muskoka Free Hospital opened, but it would only accept patients in the early stages of the disease. It was not until 1904 that patients who were chronically sick but couldn't afford to pay for their care were catered for, with the opening of the Toronto Free Hospital for Consumptive Poor. The 'Poor' was dropped soon after the hospital was opened[95], even though it was built especially for those who could not manage to pay. The hospital had capacity for up to 115 patients.

Toronto Free Hospital for Consumptives c1930. Postcard: Unknown

Like most home-based crafts, basket making was not a very lucrative occupation so Arthur would not have had much money when he left England in 1903. There is a strong likelihood that he would have been fairly poor and living in less than desirable conditions. Mixing closely with others in the same situation, he would have been a prime target for tuberculosis bacteria.

Sure enough, Arthur contracted the disease and took a turn for the worse in August 1907, when he was admitted to the Toronto Free Hospital for Consumptives.

Dr. William James Dobbie, Arthur's physician at the hospital, was a renowned expert in the field. Not only was he the physician in charge at the hospital, he is credited with many papers including one in The Public Health Journal, Toronto, 1921 entitled The Etiology of Tuberculosis[96].

Despite Dr. Dobbie's expertise, recovery from tuberculosis was rare at the time. Although Arthur fought the disease for more than two years, he died on the 9th November 1909. His death record confirms that when he was admitted to the hospital he was still working as a basket maker, the trade he had learnt after leaving home for Lake Street in Leighton Buzzard back in 1900.

Arthur never married.

Frederick

Frederick, known to most as Fred, was just thirteen when he left home. He moved in with his sister Rosa Odell at their house in Thompson Street, Bradwell. Fred's occupation is given as Grocer in the 1901 census and it is likely that he worked as a delivery boy at one of the Co-op stores, one of which opened on New Bradwell High Street in 1869[97]. If not there, just around the corner on Old Bradwell Road there was a small grocery store which would have been very convenient for Fred and could have been where he worked.

Fred and Tom turned up at the same recruiting station at the same time on the same day and signed up to the same regiment, the King's Royal Rifle Corps. They had consecutive army numbers and spent the first years of their military careers together. It would be a travesty not to include a summary of Fred's British Army and WW1 exploits in this memoir.

Although Tom took part in many battles before being wounded and captured at Ypres in November 1914, he was relatively safe for the remainder of the war. He endured the hardship of prisoner of war camps, had to fight the temptation to escape and risk being shot, and suffered the humiliation of being held under control of a foreign power. Fred, on the other hand, would be courting death on a regular basis fighting at the Western Front until 1917 when he was shelled at Arras. He was stretchered to England on the 19th April that year for hospital treatment for the fourth and last time. He was never to return to the Front, but his final months in the British Army would leave him with much more than physical scars.

Fred's first medical examination after attestation shows that he was much slighter in build than Tom. Although he was half an inch taller, his weight was only 118 pounds, which is a stone and a half lighter than his brother. His chest measurement was 31 inches compared to Tom's 36 inches. Fred was two years and four months younger than Tom, which could account for some of the difference. His physical development was considered only fair, and his complexion was described as sallow. Fred's eyes were light grey and his hair dark brown, the only details that match those of his brother.

Frederick Wadner. Photo: Courtesy of Bob Webber

Fred and Tom were posted to the same locations for the first few years after they signed up. They travelled together on the HT Dunera to Malta in 1904, on the HS Dilwara to Crete in 1905 and for a second voyage on the HT Dunera on the 1st March 1906, this time to Cairo in Egypt. It was there that the brothers parted company for a while, with Fred heading for a two year stay in Khartoum, Sudan while Tom remained in Cairo. Fred returned to Cairo on the 3rd May 1908 to be hospitalised with gastric catarrh. The brothers were reunited and on the 29th January 1909 they boarded the HS Braemar Castle which was to take them back to Gosport, arriving in England on the 12th February 1909.

Fred was promoted from rifleman to lance corporal in 1905, granted 1G.C. (One Good Conduct) Badge in 1906 and was promoted to corporal on the 1st April 1909. Six months later in October 1909, he was found absent from canteen duty and was severely reprimanded. He was similarly punished a year later for creating a disturbance in his Company's barracks at 10:40pm. Neither of these were serious offences, but on the 29th September 1910 he left guard duty without orders from his superior officer and was reduced to the ranks. The same fate had befallen Tom in 1907, when he was reduced from lance corporal to the rank of rifleman for misconduct.

On the 9th December 1911, after eight years service, Fred transferred to the Army Reserve. He took a job as a railway porter at Avonmouth, a suburb of Bristol. It was there that he met Ada Ford. Ada had been widowed in 1911 when her husband of six years William Elliott died suddenly at the age of 31 from a ruptured heart aneurism, leaving her with three young children to care for. Fred and Ada married at Bristol Register Office on the 22nd February 1913, and moved into 4 Stephen Street not far from where Ada and William had lived at Tuckers Court. Their first-born, Arthur, who arrived a couple of months later, was to die from diarrhoeal disease at only four months old on the 2nd September 1913.

Fred was recalled to the 1st Battalion KRRC and mobilised at Winchester on the 5th August 1914, the day after war was declared on Germany. He joined the British Expeditionary Force in France on the 12th August. On the 14th August at Hanappes in the Ardennes,

Fred was appointed lance corporal (unpaid). He fought at Mons, Marne and at Aisne and was commissioned for services in the field on the 11th October 1914, although the promotion was not to reach his Commanding Officer until the 22nd. He was promoted to 2nd lieutenant at the same time as Tom.

Extract from original War Diary 22nd October 1914. Image: The National Archives[98] (OGL)

Between the Battle of the Aisne in September 1914 and the First Battle of Ypres which commenced on the 19th October, there was sporadic fighting between the Germans and the BEF. Fred was very severely wounded in action on the 13th October 1914 when his right thigh was splintered by a shell casing delivered from heavy artillery.

Extract from original War Diary 13th October 1914. Image: The National Archives[99] (OGL)

It appears that the Commanding Officer mixed up the two brothers, because the war diary records that it was T. Wadner who sustained the shell wound. Tom, though, sustained a bullet wound to the arm when he was captured on the 2nd November. It was probably quite unusual for brothers to be fighting in the same unit, so a slip of the pen is perhaps unsurprising.

In one sense it was fortunate that Fred was badly wounded. Had he taken part in the next round of major fighting at Ypres commencing just one week later, he could well have been captured alongside his brother. Fred was taken from the field by stretcher before sailing back to Southampton from Le Havre on HS Oxfordshire and admitted to the 3rd Southern General Hospital, Oxford[100]. A Medical Board held on the 22nd March 1915 found Fred to be fit only for light duty at home. He was first posted to the 3rd (Reserve) Battalion KRRC at Witley Camp, and then on the 3rd April 1915 to the 5th (Reserve) Battalion KRRC at Fort Grain, Isle of Grain in Kent. The 5th (Reserve) was a depot and training unit. On the 11th May 1915, whilst still receiving treatment, Fred was promoted to the rank of lieutenant.

The wound sustained just before Ypres took a full year to heal, and Fred was not considered fit for general service until the 25th October 1915. He returned to the front line at Loos, attached to the 2nd Battalion KRRC, 2nd Brigade, 1st Division. On the 30th June 1916, the Battalion was in place ready to play its part in the 'Attack on the Triangle', located in front of the Double Crassier, two huge slag-heaps.

The Double Crassier in 1918. Photo: Project Gutenburg[101]

The raid was a diversionary attack prior to the main Somme offensive planned to commence the following day. Shortly after the KRRC were in position, the Germans opened fire on the trenches and caused heavy losses. Five officers were killed and six wounded, and 227 other ranks were either killed, wounded or missing[102]. Fred was one of the injured officers, sustaining wounds in ten places. He was transported from the battlefield on the 1st July, and left Calais for Dover on the 7th July 1916.

Although none of Fred's wounds were as severe as the previous shrapnel wound to his thigh, he had to suffer a series of operations, the last of which was on the 3rd January 1917. Promoted to the rank of captain on the 1st January 1917, he was posted to the 1st Battalion KRRC and returned to the Front in February 1917 prior to the first Battle of Arras. Four days into the battle, on the 13th April, Fred was hit by a shell which took a slice from his left leg and resulted in compound fractures of his left tibia. Five others were wounded by the same shell, and a 2nd lieutenant and one rifleman were killed outright. In spite of his injury and the constant shelling, he remained with his Company in the front line overnight between 7:50 in the evening and 8:00 the following morning. A letter written by Fred on the 16th June 1918 states, 'This certainly shook my nerves up a little.' That seems a gross understatement, considering he spent twelve hours in darkness, with shells raining down around his position.

Fred was stretchered from the field to Calais, where on the 19th April 1917 he embarked on HS Cambria bound for Dover.

SS Cambria. Photo: Postcard Unknown

Fred's injury at Arras was to be the end of his participation in Europe. After leaving hospital on the 18th July 1917, he was posted to Aldershot to help form a new Battalion, the 97th Training Reserve. The Battalion's Commanding Officer reported that Fred was 'efficient in every way and full of zeal in the command of his Company.'

However, by the end of August, it was noticed that Fred was no longer showing his usual efficiency, and on more than one occasion he was instructed to return to his quarters after being suspected of having drunk too much. After inspection of Fred's mess bills his new Commanding Officer told him that the excessive drinking must end. There was a further written report that Fred was over-indulging, causing his character to change from being quiet and observant with attention to detail, to becoming argumentative and having some difficulty in grasping what was being said to him. On the 17th October 1917, he was relieved from duty for being under the influence and his Commanding Officer requested that he be removed from the Battalion.

The Army Council investigated the case, and for a while they seriously considered proceeding with a Court Martial. However, because of the lenient way the offences had previously been dealt with, and particularly because Fred was never formally put under arrest, the Army Council recommended that he be called upon to resign his Commission. This he was instructed to do by letter on the 12th December 1917, and he signed his resignation on the 18th December 1917. Throughout the proceedings, Fred insisted that he was innocent, and that the charges were the result of his new Commanding Officer taking a deep dislike to him.

During the months that followed, Fred wrote to the authorities several times regarding his forced resignation from the army. His final appeal found its way to the highest authorities, and was given due consideration by Winston Churchill. Churchill became Secretary of State for War and Air in January 1919, and perhaps might have had a deep understanding of Fred's situation. He had, after all, experienced the horrors of the Western Front on a number of occasions while commanding the 6th Battalion, Royal Scots Fusiliers.

However, it appears that understanding was not forthcoming, and Fred gave up his fight for justice after receiving a letter from Churchill's Private Secretary. The letter informed him that his case had been carefully considered, but Churchill was unable to recommend any change to the Army Council's decision. The letter is dated the 18th June 1919. Sidney Herbert, who signed the letter as Churchill's Private Secretary, was to become Parliamentary Private Secretary to the Prime Minister, Stanley Baldwin, in 1923.

Letter from the Secretary of State for War. Image: The National Archives[103] (OGL)

Fred's only remaining option would have been to exercise his right of Petition to the King as an ordinary citizen, but he probably didn't know he could do that. In any case, it would have been a daunting step to have taken.

There were at least 80,000 cases of shell shock recorded by the end of the war. Increasingly it was realised that it could be set off by more than physical trauma, with psychological causes also to blame. Significantly, shell shock was found to affect about five times more officers than men in the ranks. At no time did anyone suggest that Fred's change in behaviour could have been the result of shell shock, but it seems a very likely connection. There are no reports in the 196 pages of military records available from The National Archives that Fred was ever seen drunk, and the case against him appears to have been built around the amount of alcohol he was buying in the officer's mess rather than the amount he was drinking.

After Fred completed his initial military service after eight years in the army, his transfer document to the Army Reserve states clearly that his conduct had been 'Very good - no instances of drunkenness', and his character as 'Thoroughly sober and trustworthy.' It is hard not to recall Fred's words after returning wounded from the Battle of Arras, 'This certainly shook my nerves up a little'.

Because of the circumstances under which he was commanded to resign his commission, Fred was not awarded a gratuity nor a retirement pension to help towards looking after his wife and children. To make matters even more difficult, he didn't have the opportunity to learn a trade while he was in the army. He was skilled in the use of weapons from musketry to machine guns, knew open and closed drill, semaphore, all about bombs and grenades, and attack and counter attack formations. As a captain, he was charged with the safety and actions of up to one hundred men under his command. None of these skills was to help him get a comparable job in civilian life, and Fred had little choice after leaving the army but to resume his earlier career with the railways.

Fred and Ada were to have seven children of their own with military regularity. Gladys was born on the 17th September, 1915 almost exactly two years after Arthur, who died as a baby. Arthur George, Thomas, John Cade, Victor Frederick and Rosa followed at two year intervals.

During the six years following his resignation from the army, Fred spent many weeks in hospital having operations to improve the wounds he sustained at the Front. It is said that in 1924, a large piece of shrapnel was removed from his leg together with fragments of his clothing attached to it. This would probably have been from the Battle of Arras in April 1917, which was the last time he was wounded.

Fred continued to work for the Great Western Railway as a cleaner, and in 1939 at the age of 52 was still living with Ada at their original home in Stephen Street[104].

In spite of any enmity he might have felt after being forced to resign his army commission, Fred joined his local Home Guard when WW2 broke out. Because of the Bristol Aeroplane Company's site at Filton, and the ease with which enemy bombers could follow the River Avon to the heart of the city at night, Bristol was the fifth most heavily bombed location in Britain. Fred will have been kept very busy keeping people safe from unexploded bombs.

Fred died from a cerebral haemorrhage on the 6th December 1956 at the age of 69 in Bathavon just four years after retiring from the railways as a foreman in the Goods Department. Ada was living at 50 Kenmore Crescent, Bristol when she died aged 75 on the 17th April 1960 at Manor Park Hospital, Bristol.

Fred in WW2, and Fred and Ada Wadner Gravestone. Photos: Courtesy of Bob Webber

The Middle Years

Violet Winifred Attersall - Tom's Wife

Violet Winifred Attersall, who some twenty three years later would become Tom's wife and life-long partner, was born on the 8th December 1890 just off the Old Kent Road. In 1891 at three months old she lived at 113 Avondale Square, North Camberwell, London with her father John (41), mother Jane Ann née Asquith (38) and four brothers, Albert (16) and Horace (14) both office boys, Archibald (7) and Reuben (2). The area was blitzed in 1940 during WW2 and has been completely redeveloped. None of the old buildings is still standing, and even the church was bombed and had to be demolished, although it was re-built in 1963.

Original St Philips Church, Avondale Square. Photo: Postcard Unknown

John Attersall was an Assistant Superintendant Telegraph Clerk at the Central Telegraph Office just across the river on Newgate Street, and the family lived at 51 Clifton Crescent in Peckham when he died of a perforated stomach ulcer in 1897 at the age of forty five. The death was registered by John's son Horace, who was present at the death. John left his wife £243.16s.4d in his Will, the equivalent of about £30,000 today. Violet was six when her father died, and by 1901 when she was ten years old she and her mother Jane (who had recorded her age on the census as forty when in fact she would have been forty eight) had moved to South Stoneham in Southampton where she ran a general store on Langhorn Road.

Around the corner from Langhorn Road, 1901. Photo: Old S'ton - A Pictorial Memory[105]

The reason they chose Southampton was probably because Jane's sister Henrietta and her husband George Harper lived there at 17 Melbourne Street. Violet's older brother Horace, a ship's steward, also lived in Southampton when he was not at sea, boarding with his aunt and uncle. Although staying with them in 1901, sadly Horace died later that year in Peckham, aged twenty four. His death certificate records the cause of death as haemoptysis suffocative / phthisis pulmonalis which in layman's terms means he probably had tuberculosis. He was buried at Southwark Cemetery on the 23rd October 1901.

By 1906, Henrietta and George had taken over the licence of the Dorset Arms in Orchard Lane, Southampton. Their pub was to be the scene of a tragedy worse than the loss of Horace at such a young age. On the 18th November 1906, Henrietta's and George's daughter (and Violet's cousin) Beatrice was murdered by her estranged husband William Owen at the Dorset Arms when he took a razor to her throat[106]. After two years of marriage to William, Beatrice had left the matrimonial home to live with her parents at the pub. The immediate aftermath was witnessed by them and also by Violet's brothers Archibald and Albert, who were visiting their uncle and aunt. The newspaper reports of the murder are quite graphic and best not repeated here. Beatrice was only twenty four years old, the same as Horace when he died. William Owen was sentenced to death and was to be hanged at Winchester prison on the 25th March 1907. However, the Home Secretary intervened after a public petition was raised in his defence, and four days before the execution the sentence was commuted to one of penal servitude for life[107]. He died in 1947 at the age of seventy.

There is no sign of Jane's general store on recent maps. It was situated between numbers 3 and 4 Langhorn Road, but the area must have been extensively redeveloped as the present houses appear to be more recent. None of the occupants living between numbers 1 and 11 Langhorn Road in the 1901 census is listed at the same property in 1911. In September 1906, 'Six well-arranged houses with long gardens being Nos. 1-6 Langhorn Road' were put up for auction, according to a notice in the Hampshire Advertiser[108].

Langhorn Road, date unknown. Photo: Postcard Unknown.

The houses shown on the postcard may have replaced the original six which were present on the north side of the road in 1906. An 1892 map of the road has just six large houses on the northern side, but a 1910 map shows a row of about twenty in their place. All of this points towards the probability that the houses and the general store were demolished. The first few years of the 1900s were certainly not good ones for Violet or her mother.

There are no 1911 census records for Violet, who would have turned twenty in that year. It is quite possible that she might have been protesting at not being allowed to vote in government elections. Her mother's maiden name of Asquith could offer more weight to that possibility, although there is no evidence of a family link to the prime minister of the day. Tens of thousands of disenfranchised women took the opportunity to demonstrate their disapproval of Herbert Asquith's Liberal government's lack of reform concerning women's suffrage by refusing to fill out their census forms on the night of 2nd April 1911. Some simply refused, some spent the night walking around away from home, some wrote protest messages on their form and some simply hid when the enumerator called.

Suffrage in Southampton, 1911. Photo: Unknown[109]

The 1901 census is the last known record of Violet for twelve years. Because women did not have the same right to vote as men until 1928, neither Violet nor her mother Jane appear on the electoral registers of the time. Jane is recorded in 1911 as a domestic servant living and working for the Haviland family at 108 Lowther Road, Bournemouth, but there is no mention of Violet. Jane was still not being entirely truthful about her age, which is recorded as forty eight instead of fifty eight, her actual age. She must have maintained much of her youthful looks to have got away with it.

So, after her husband's death in 1897, Jane picked herself up and made a life for Violet at the general store in Southampton. But clearly sometime between 1901 and 1911 her luck ran out, she and Violet were no longer living together, and at the age of fifty eight Jane was reduced to working as a servant.

Jane must have returned to Southampton, because that is where she suffered a fatal stroke on the 25th July 1927 at the age of seventy four. The address where she died is given on her death certificate as 1a Chilworth Road, Southampton. This was a euphemistic address for the Southampton Workhouse Union Infirmary, used to avoid embarrassment on birth and death certificates. Her nephew Albert's wife Gertrude, living in Southampton at 42 Chapel Road at the time, certified the death giving Jane's occupation as 'of 26 Cable Street, widow of John Attersall, Telegraphist'. That seems an odd way of describing Jane's occupation, particularly as her husband died thirty years earlier, but might have seemed better than the truth. The 1925 Kelly's directory for Southampton has one Frederick William Haynes living at that address, but there are no instances of Attersall or Asquith in the directory. All of the houses in Cable Street have been replaced by industrial units.

Sadly, it appears that Jane probably died a pauper.

Marriage

How did Tom and Violet meet? There doesn't appear to be any prior link to the Attersall or Asquith families in the Bedford area, and although Violet was living at the general store in 1901 when she was ten years old, there are no records which confirm her whereabouts until her marriage to Tom twelve years later. It would seem likely that Violet and Tom met while she was living in Southampton and Tom was located either at Gosport or Aldershot.

On the 2nd April 1911, Tom was stationed at Alverstoke, a small area of Gosport about 20 miles from Southampton. He was posted to Aldershot in November of that year, about 45 miles from Southampton. Between the 12th and the 30th March 1912, he was in the Military Isolation Hospital at Aldershot, about a quarter of a mile from the Cambridge Military Hospital, with a case of mumps. There was no mumps vaccine until 1948, and the virus was prevalent in adults as well as children before then. Tom might not have thought it at the time, but at least he received the best possible treatment before returning to civilian life in 1913 and he would never catch mumps again.

Military Hospital, Aldershot. Photo: Postcard Unknown

A fairy tale writer might cast Violet as a nurse at the Military Hospital where Tom was in isolation recovering from his case of mumps. She could have joined the Queen Alexandra's Imperial Military Nursing

Service, or the Red Cross, although sadly no search results surface with them, nor at The National Archives. It would, indeed, just be a fairy tale.

The marriage certificate describes Tom's 'Rank or Profession' as labourer and his residence as North Wingfield. This is puzzling, because there is no correlation between his residence in North Wingfield, which is in Derbyshire, and his army addresses. There was an Army Reserve Unit at Chesterfield, not far away, but there is nothing in Tom's army record to suggest he was involved in anything there. Only five months passed between him transferring to the Reserve of Officers and his marriage at Ravensden, so it would make more sense if he had returned to his home ground around Bedford. We will probably never discover what he was doing in Derbyshire. Violet's residence, on the other hand, is given as Ravensden on the marriage certificate. There is no indication of her actual address although it is a fair assumption that she was living with Tom's mother Amelia, and Jimmy Jones.

The marriage banns were read three times in the parish of North Wingfield between the 8th and the 22nd June 1913, and must also have been read in the parish of Ravensden. There is a note that the certificate permitting the marriage was issued on the 23rd June 1913, allowing the ceremony to go ahead the next day.

Tom and Violet's Marriage Banns. Image: Derbyshire Record Office, D1434/A/PI/4/9[110]

Tom and Violet were married on the 24th June 1913 at All Saints Church in Ravensden. Witnesses at the wedding were Tom's brother Jim, and his step-brother Charles Jones.

All Saints Church, Ravensden, Photo: Hilary and Nigel Worker

Chapel Yard, Ravensden

Jimmy Jones lived at Chapel Yard from around 1880, and it is there that Tom's mother Amelia joined him and his family after their marriage in 1900.

Chapel Yard is unmarked. It is tucked away behind what is now Ravensden Baptist Church, and accessed via Chapel Lane which joins Oldway Road about 200 yards from what is locally known as the Ravensden Crossroads. In 1911 there were seven people living there, four male and three female[111], which would tie in with the Bedfordshire council tax record that lists three buildings in Chapel Yard: Laburnum Cottage, and two others at number two and number three. A 1900 map shows the cottages, and three more buildings scattered further down the yard which have since been demolished. These were probably outbuildings which Jimmy Jones might have used for his business, or by other occupants of the cottages in the course of theirs.

Chapel House and Chapel Lane, Ravensden. Photo: Google Streetview

The Ravensden village website has a 'Who's Who in Ravensden in 1965' page[112] which includes a Mrs. Fensome at Laburnum Cottage. She was the village's oldest inhabitant at ninety three. Jane Fensome appears in the 1911 census living in Chapel Road (probably Chapel Yard). Her husband Frank ran his own business as a wheelwright from their cottage, and also living there were their five children. Next door to Jane Fensome in 1911, lived Tom's mother Amelia and his step-father Jimmy Jones. Tom would certainly have known Mrs. Fensome, who would have been aged about forty seven in 1919. He would probably also have been on speaking terms with the chapel caretaker, who in 1911 was Mary Ann Peacock and who lived at Chapel House, the cottage facing Oldway Road.

What is not known for certain, is where Violet was living before her marriage. Did she just give Ravensden as her address because she had travelled up from the Southampton area for the wedding and was staying for a short time at Chapel Yard? Or maybe if she did meet Tom when he was stationed at Gosport, he might have suggested that she move to Ravensden quite a long time before, perhaps while he was working in North Wingfield.

The 1918 and 1919 electoral rolls give Tom's address as Chapel Yard, Ravensden but record him as an 'Absent Voter'. That means Amelia and Jimmy Jones were most likely at Chapel Yard in 1919, and it is a fair assumption that Violet would have been living with them while Tom was a prisoner of war, together with four year old daughter Joy. Betty was not born until the end of 1919, but Violet would have been pregnant with her while living at the cottage.

Numbers 2 and 1 Chapel Lane (Chapel Yard), Ravensden. Photos: Hilary and Nigel Worker

Gladstone Street, Bedford

Tom's permanent address after he had been repatriated from Germany appears in his army records about a dozen times as 119 Gladstone Street, Bedford. The first is a letter from Tom to the War Office dated the 14th September 1919 asking for information regarding his request to resign his commission, and mentioning that he was on leave. The last is a letter from the War Office on the 2nd January 1920 approving Tom's retirement from the army.

119 Gladstone Street, Bedford Present Day. Photo: Google Streetview

In April 1911, the house was occupied by a large family comprising Mrs. Shawe, a widow of private means, two daughters, her daughter-in-law and two grandchildren. The house would have been more than large enough for Tom, Violet and four year old Joy so there is a good chance that they just rented rooms.

119 Gladstone Street would have been the first accommodation that Tom and Violet could call their own home following their marriage in 1913. Their daughter Betty was born there at the end of 1919, which might have prompted the growing family to look for somewhere with more space. In 1920, Tom took a position as groom on South Pillinge Farm at Marston Moretaine just outside Bedford. The job included a cottage, but Tom was not to keep his position for long.

Marston Moretaine

South Pillinge Farm was situated close to Marston Moretaine about a quarter of a mile north east of Millbrook Station on the L&NWR Bedford Branch railway line.

South Pillinge Farm, Millbrook. Photo: Google Maps

The farm is still there today, with the famous Millbrook Proving Ground for motor vehicles almost next door. Tom worked at the farm as horse keeper until August 1920, and in October of that year the family was still living in a tied cottage nearby known as Cottage No. 1.

South Pillinge Farm was administered by the Duke of Bedford's estate, and Charles Hall of Park Farm Office, Woburn requested on 12th October 1920 that Tom be evicted from the cottage as it was needed by the farm tenant Mr. Gilbert for the new horse keeper[113].

The secretary of the Bedfordshire Agricultural Executive Committee responded on the 13th October with a number of queries which would have taken some time to answer, so it seems likely that the family was able to remain until they moved into The Polhill Arms in November 1920. Strangely, the 1922 electoral register still records Tom and Violet living in the cottage, but this must simply have been an administrative error.

The Polhill Arms

The Polhill Arms at Salph End, Renhold was acquired by Higgins & Sons Ltd., Bedford in 1851. The Higgins brothers tried to sell the company in 1927 when expansion ground to a halt, but it took until 1931 before they succeeded. On the 21st September 1931, Wells & Winch of Biggleswade bought the company, together with all of its public houses, for £180,000[114].

Thomas Pettit was licensee for ten years between 1904 and 1914, after which there were four different licensees each only running the pub for one or two years until Tom took over the license in 1920.

It might appear on the surface that becoming a publican was a strange choice to make for a new career at the age of thirty five. Renhold, though, is close to Goldington Highfields where Tom had lived on and off before joining the army in 1904, and that could have been one factor in the equation. Another might be that after sixteen years in the army, four of them spent in a prisoner of war camp, Tom could have found returning to agriculture an unattractive proposition, and might even have seen working as a groom or labouring a bit *infra dig* for a retired captain.

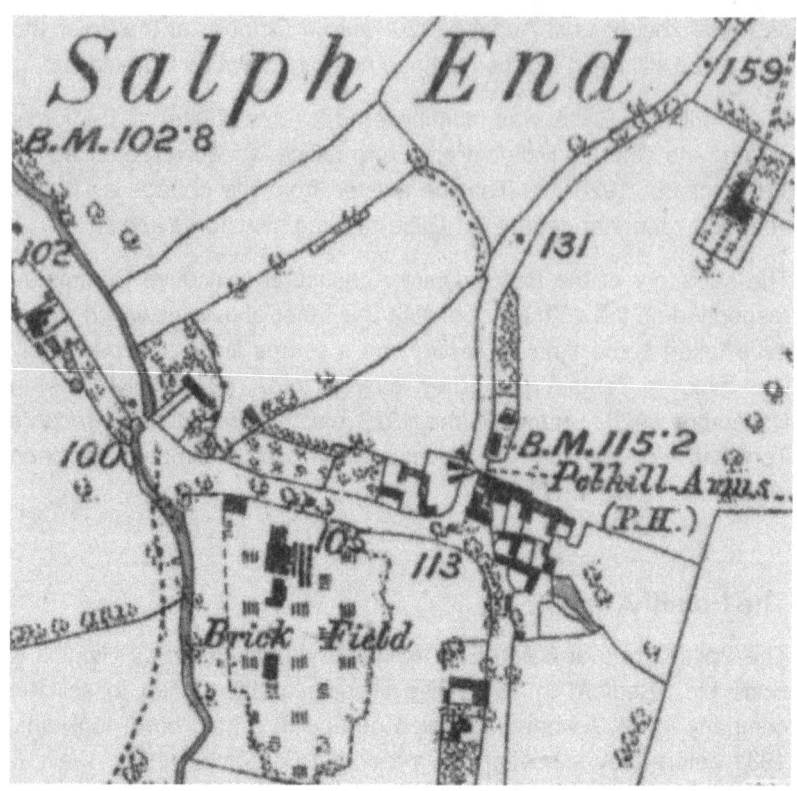

Salph End, Renhold, 1884 - The Polhill Arms. Map: National Library of Scotland

The overriding factor would probably have been that Tom needed a more permanent home for himself, Violet and daughters Joy, then five years old and Betty, aged just one. They had been living temporarily at 119 Gladstone Street and then for almost a year at the tied cottage in Marston Moretaine.

The war years had not been kind to publicans or to breweries. Men had left the villages to fight for their country, and beer production had been halved by the Government because it was seen as unnecessary to the war effort. The strength of beer had been watered down to about half in an effort to maintain an adequate supply, and excise tax had risen significantly resulting in a considerable increase in the price of a pint[115].

In 1900, a pint of ale cost around 3d in pre-decimalisation money. It increased to about 4d when war broke out in 1914 and steadily rose to 10d by the end of the war[116]. Customers in rural areas such as Bedfordshire would not have been able to afford such prices, even though 10d was less than a five pence piece today, and this might be one reason that the turnover of licensees during those times was very high. Judging by the number of advertisements 'To Let' that appeared in the Bedfordshire Times, Wells & Winch were having difficulty finding people willing to take on a new license. Tom will doubtless have seen the one placed on the 10th September 1920.

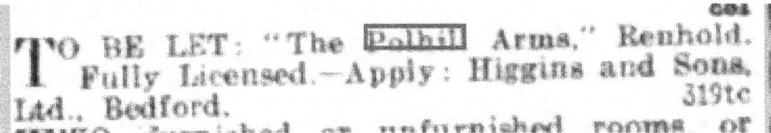

Classified Section from The Bedfordshire Times and Independent 10th September 1920

He applied to take over the pub and moved in with his family in early November 1920.

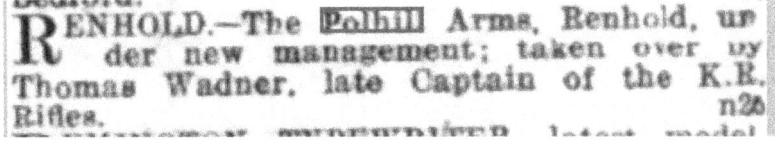

Classified Section from The Bedfordshire Times and Independent 19th November 1920

The Land Valuation Act of 1925 required the value of every property in the country to be established to assess the rates required to be paid to the government. The Polhill Arms was included in the valuation, and the field notes that were taken during the valuation officer's visit include many details of not only the property, but its contents[117].

Tom was cited as the occupier of the pub, with a note that he had been at The Polhill Arms for seven years and that it was a 'Good house but poor trade'. The surveyor also noted that the 'Publican seems a popular sort'. There is no date on the hand-written notes, but the survey must have been taken in 1927 because Tom took over the license in 1920. He was on a monthly tenure, and the rent was £25. It was noted that in 1920 the rent was £12, so more than doubling it over seven years was a significant increase.

According to the surveyor's notes, the public areas comprised a tap room, a small smoke room, a cellar and an outside urinal. Private areas included a lounge, scullery and pantry with three bedrooms upstairs. No mention was made of a separate kitchen downstairs, or a bathroom upstairs. Outside were noted two privies, a coal barn, dairy and a corn loft. Farm buildings were also noted, and included two hen houses, two stables, two cart hovels and a water well.

A stock take also took place as part of the survey, and there is a list of items held. Some are priced per item but others, such as cigarettes, sweets and crisps, show the total stock. These are trade prices, so for instance the bitter at 4/8d per gallon would work out at 7d per pint cost price. That left the brewery 3d profit before other expenses.

TRADE	
3 dozen Bass and Guinness 7d.	36 gallons mild 3/4d
3½ dozen minerals 2½d.	18 gallons bitter 4/8d
1 bottle whisky 13/4d.	1/2 bottle rum 13/4d
1 bottle gin 13/4d.	1 bottle brandy 17/6d
3 bottles port 4/6d.	1½ oz tobacco 10d/oz.
Cigarettes 37/-. Sweets 4/-.	Crisps 6/-

Stock Transcribed from Valuation Notes 1927

The land surrounding the pub was estimated to be 3.827 in area, but there is no indication of the unit used. If it is acres, that would be around 16,000 square yards, which as a square would measure about 125 yards along each edge. Looking at the 1900 map for The Polhill Arms, if the land includes some of the adjacent fields, four acres could be correct.

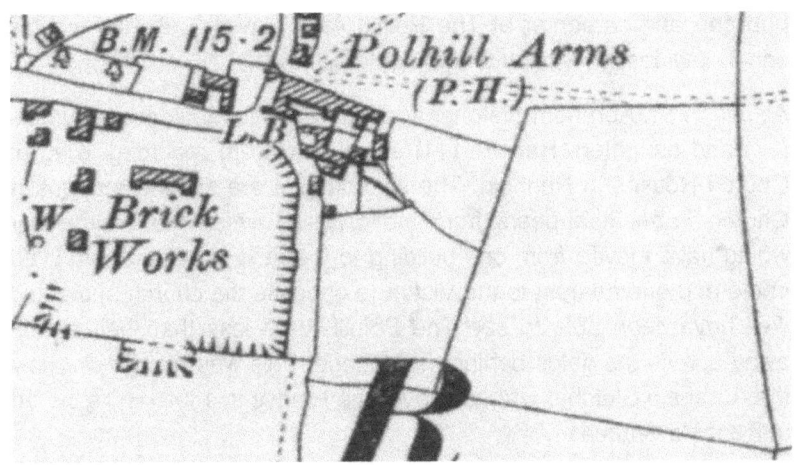

The Polhill Arms Map c 1900. Map: National Library of Scotland

Previous licensees of the Polhill Arms are listed on a plaque in the bar, and Tom is shown there between 1920 and 1927.

Polhill Arms Plaque. Photo: Paul Smith

James Sletcher, the first recorded licensee, is shown on the 1881 census as a widower (his wife Mary died in 1880) aged seventy three, publican and carpenter at The Polhill Arms. Living with him are his son-in-law Joseph Money and daughter Emma.

Also in 1881, Abraham Sletcher aged 38, his wife Matilda née Lumbis (37) and daughters Hannah (11) and Ada (7) are recorded living at Church Houses in Renhold. The six cottages are still there opposite Church Farm. It appears from the order in which the enumerator would have moved from one building to the next, that Abraham lived in the end one nearest to the Vicarage opposite the church and could well have been able to see The Polhill Arms less than half a mile away across the fields behind the cottage. This was almost certainly the Abraham Sletcher who took over the license in 1890. He is buried at Renhold Church.

This 1894 photograph of the pub shows members of the Pedley family who were next in line for the license.

Polhill Arms 1894. Photo: Courtesy of Paul Smith, with thanks to the Pedley Family

The building looks much the same from the outside today as it did in Victorian times. The pub sign has been replaced, but it still shows the original Polhill family coat of arms. Although not shown in the photograph, the chimneys above the open range in the bar were originally tall ones, and have been replaced.

The post box in the wall has been removed, but it would have been there when Tom was licensee. The post was collected at 8:45 am, 11:25 am, 2:30 pm and 5:20 pm unless it was a Sunday, in which case there was just one collection at 10:35 am. The wall boxes at Top End and Water End were only cleared twice each day, late morning and late afternoon. There was a ten minute interval between the collection times at the different boxes so it must have taken about that for the postman to cycle between each one.

Imagine Tom popping out the front to post this letter he wrote to the War Office confirming his new address.

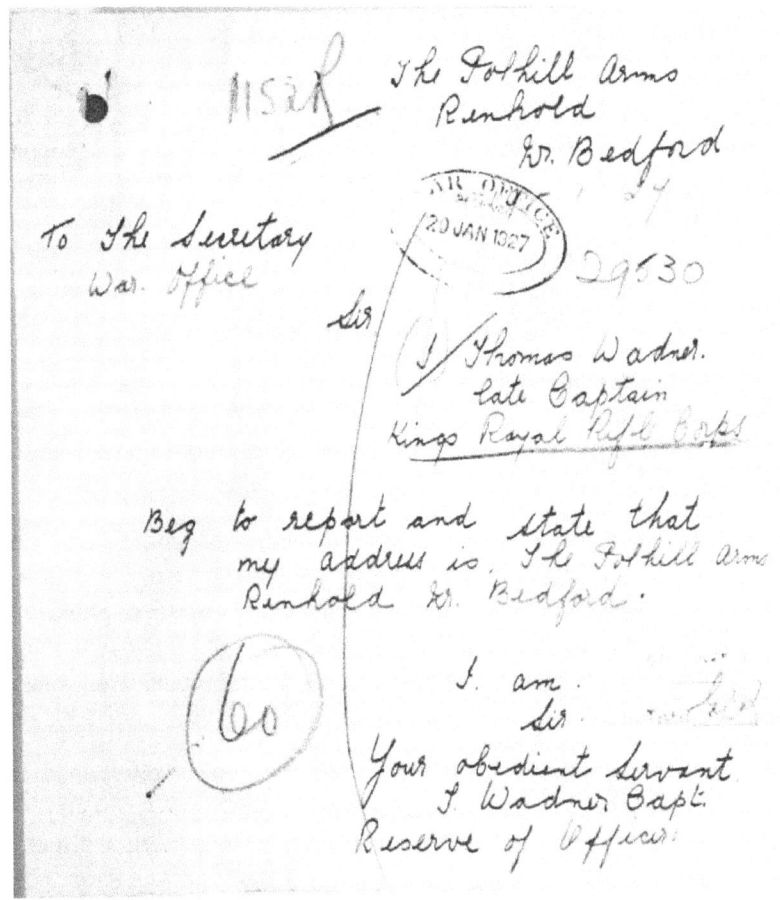

Letter from Tom to The War Office 1927. Image: The National Archives[118] (OGL)

When the 1894 photograph of The Polhill Arms was taken, Tom was aged nine and lived about two miles away at Highfields Farm, Goldington. The accident at Jackman's Farm that killed his father Arthur would occur two years later in 1896. There is an interesting connection here. Abraham Sletcher's wife Matilda had a brother John Lumbis born in 1852 at Union House, Bedford otherwise known as the Bedford Union Workhouse, on Kimbolton Road. John Lumbis and his wife Ruth bore nine children, one of whom was Arthur Joseph Lumbis in 1875. Arthur Joseph Lumbis, Abraham Sletcher's nephew, was almost certainly the same man that Tom's father died trying to rescue from the cess pit at Jackman's Farm on 3rd June 1896. It would be extraordinary if there was not at least a tenuous link between the two families.

Three of Tom's children were born while he and Violet ran the pub. Arthur Peter was the first, on the 10th January 1923. Then John Edward, the author's father, on the 23rd September 1924 followed by David Thomas on the 16th August 1926. Even Peter, though, would hardly remember living there as he was only four years old when they moved on. It is doubtful that John or David, who were only three and one when they left, would have had any recollection at all.

The accommodation would have been a tight squeeze for a family of seven. Upstairs, the pub was quite small, and the private lounge was downstairs together with a shared kitchen. Each room had an open fire, which was the usual form of heating at the time.

Tom's daughter Joy was five years old when they moved to The Polhill Arms, and would probably have attended the Boys and Girls School at Church End at the junction with Wood Drive, about halfway between the church and The Three Horseshoes pub. Betty would not have been old enough until around 1924, but could well have attended between then and when the family left the village in 1927.

The establishment was a Church of England school which opened in 1866[119]. It cost £735 and was designed to take 120 children[120]. Counting the names recorded as scholars in 1881 for Renhold there were 102 in the village, so the school would have been well-attended.

Boys and Girls School, Wood Drive, Renhold. Photo: Google Streetview

Prior to 1866, there was a much smaller 'Daily School' which in 1833 contained 28 boys and 8 girls. That is a low percentage for a population of 453 in that year, and ties in with the poor level of literacy at the time[121].

Like most agricultural communities throughout the 19th and early 20th centuries, Renhold was rarely in the headlines. When local tragedy struck, though, The Polhill Arms often featured as the venue for inquests. One such occasion was when three year old Phoebe Cox fell into Renhold brook and drowned on the 31st January 1862[122]. Another was when George Pedley, landlord at The Polhill Arms between 1903-1904, hanged himself in a barn at the pub[123]. James Sletcher was often in the news for having his license refused, or suffering a short ban on trading, mostly following a fracas or for allowing fighting at the pub[124].

Not to escape notoriety, Tom was found guilty of trespass on the 2nd September 1926. He spotted some partridges in a field off Wilden Road, cycled up with a gun under his arm, crept down under a hedge and shot one of the birds. He was seen recovering the bird by the local gamekeeper and prosecuted at Bedford Magistrates Court. The prosecutor pointed out that the defendant was the village publican, and if he was allowed to get away with poaching what chance was there of stopping it in the village? Tom was found guilty and fined one pound. He paid the fine in threepenny pieces[125].

Tom kept chickens in the yard at the back of the pub. He won 1st Prize for brown eggs at the Renhold Show when it was held opposite The Three Horseshoes in August 1923. The show had to be re-arranged from the Summer Bank Holiday on the 6th August until later in the month because of an outbreak of Foot and Mouth[126].

He might have spent most of the Roaring Twenties surrounded by beer and wine, but unlike London, Chicago, Berlin and Paris the nearest Tom came to 'roaring' was probably the fire in the inglenook at the end of the bar.

The license for the Polhill Arms was transferred to Joseph Stapleton on the 12th November, 1927. The price of a pint? Still the same as seven years earlier when Tom took over. 10d.

Everton

After leaving The Polhill Arms in 1927, the family moved to Everton, a small village about two miles north east of Sandy. Their address, which Tom notified to the army authorities by letter in 1927, was 2 Council Cottages, owned by Biggleswade Rural District Council. The location of 2 Council Cottages is, however, a mystery.

Along with most small rural villages, with a population of around one hundred Everton did not have named streets or house numbers until the 1930s. For those residents who did not live at a farm or in a farm cottage, or in a posh house with a name, their postal address was simply 'Everton'. Census returns scouted around the issue by giving each dwelling a number, but as cottages fell into ruin or new ones were built, there was little consistency between census years.

Following a shake-up of county boundaries, Biggleswade Rural District Council attempted to bring some order to the situation. The 1931 electoral register shows that each dwelling was allocated a number, beginning at one end of the village and ending at the other. In 1932, the council named the main thoroughfare High Street and the lane to St. Mary's church Church Road, and re-allocated each dwelling a different house number. The following year it was all changed once again, when in 1933 the road designated High Street was split into Sandy Road to the south west, and Potton Road to the south east. This would have been a time of confusion for the residents, who in the space of three years might have seen their address altered four times. For example, one house changed from Everton to 54 Everton, then to 7 High Street and finally in 1933 to 5 Sandy Road. If it was confusing for each home-owner, imagine the sleepless nights the postman must have spent.

Despite knowing the history surrounding Everton addresses, the location of Tom's house at 2 Council Cottages is very unclear. According to the Memorial Wall in Everton Village Hall, on the 31st July 1917 Private Parker Giggle was killed in action on the first day of the Third Battle of Ypres[127]. His wife Mary, and two children Ethel and Stanley, lived close by at 5 Council Cottages (although in the 1911 census, the Giggles' family address is given as 43 Everton).

Mary Giggle's address appears on the electoral register for 1936 as having changed from 5 Council Cottages to 12 Potton Road. This is the centre house of ten identically-styled semi-detached houses on the left as the village is approached from Potton. These could well have been originally known as Council Cottages, numbers 1-10. However, what is now number 12 Potton Road, counting from the edge of the village would make it number 6 Council Cottages, and Mary lived at number 5. If they were originally numbered from the centre of the village, though, the address works out correctly. Using the same approach, Tom's house at 2 Council Cottages would have been what is currently 6 Potton Road, and indeed the electoral register shows him living at that address between 1933 and 1935.

Potton Road vs Council Cottages, Everton. Photo: Google Streetview

2 Council Cottages (now 6 Potton Road), Everton. Photo: Google Streetview

There is, however, a second possibility. One of Everton's oldest residents remembers Council Cottages being in a slightly different location. Around the same time frame, three groups of six dwellings were built along the road leading from Potton Road to Gamlingay, with the first group just past the Live and Let Live public house. These cottages were picked up on the 1911 census, but given the location of 'Everton Heath, near Gamlingay'.

Being on the border between Bedfordshire, Cambridgeshire and the historical county of Huntingdonshire, slight shifts in county boundaries resulted in some confusion over the location of the parish. From 1824, there was an 'island' of Huntingdonshire within the county of Bedfordshire known locally as Donkey Island[128]. Part of Everton before 1933, including the church, overlapped Donkey Island so was located in Huntingdonshire.

'Donkey Island', Huntingdonshire in Bedfordshire 1824. Map: Wikimedia[129]

It appears that with changing county boundaries, the road out to Gamlingay which was previously Everton Heath, and now known as Everton Road, was considered by the locals to be very much a part of Everton village. If Tom's house was one of those cottages, it would have been in the nearest block to the public house.

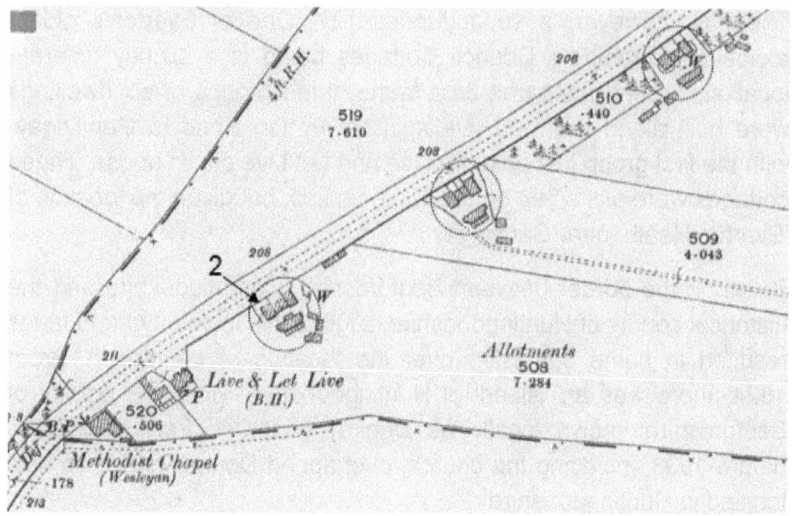

Alternative site of Council Cottages, Everton. Map: National Library of Scotland

Alternative Number 2 Council Cottages (right). Photo: Google Streetview

Of course, when Tom and the family moved to Everton in 1927, they could first have lived in the block of cottages at Everton Heath next to the Live and Let Live public house. The houses at the edge of the village in Potton Road, built by Biggleswade Rural District Council, are clearly more recent and it is possible that Tom decided to move after a year or two. There is no reason to suppose they lived in the same house all the time they were in the village, and the ever-changing addresses of the houses may have planted a red herring.

The list of Tom's known Everton addresses from various sources are not much help reaching a conclusion. The last three addresses are definitely for the same dwelling; it is only the first that is in doubt. That might have been next door to the Live and Let Live, and the others at what is now 6 Potton Road. Or they could all have been the same.

1927 to 1930: 2 Council Cottages

1931: 28 Everton

1932: 56 High St

1933 to 1935: 6 Potton Rd

Of course, the same argument would have to be applied to the Giggles family a few doors away. They would also have had to move from Council Cottages at Everton Heath to Potton Road. It is possible that they did just that, but it would have been a huge coincidence.

Wherever the exact location of Council Cottages, all of Tom's family were involved in Everton village life.

Violet (centre) at a Special Occasion in Everton. Photo: Courtesy of Sandra Edgeley

On the 17th March 1930, a meeting was held in the Schoolroom to form a branch of the British Legion in Everton. Tom was elected as one of the six committee members[130]. The branch arranged a garden fete in the grounds of Woodbury Hall the following September, where Tom was one of the gate stewards[131]. The fete raised £22. 2s. 7d.

Each year, Tom commanded the Armistice Day march. The Biggleswade Chronicle carried a report on the 16th November 1934 that on Armistice Day, the members of the British Legion set off at 1030 from the Sandy end of the village, and marched to the Memorial in the churchyard under Tom's command[132]. After the service at the memorial, the two minutes silence and the sounding of the reveille, the congregation continued to the church for the morning service.

Everton War Memorial Photo. ©2002 Martin Edwards[133]
The Thornton Arms, Everton. Photo: Google Streetview
Inside St Mary's Church, Everton. Photo: ©Mark Anderson[134]

During the 1931 County Council elections, Tom is recorded as seconding the proposed member to represent Blunham, Geoffrey Truin of High Street, Sandy[135]. There are also many records of Violet helping with teas at the village fetes, such as the one held in the Vicarage gardens on the 25th July 1935[136].

The children were often mentioned in the local paper too. David, aged eight, took part in a concert at Everton Junior School on the14th December, 1934 where he gave a recitation. He also acted in the Christmas play 'The Little Man in the Moon'[137]. Over one hundred parents and friends were watching, so Tom and Violet were almost certainly in the audience. On the 7th August 1935, the school held a Parents and Sports Day[138]. David, nine, came third in the fifty yards handicap, first in the three-legged race, second in the wheelbarrow and first in the dressing race. John, aged eleven, made third in the long jump, first in the donkey race and first in the obstacle race.

The original school dated back to 1837, but only accommodated eight pupils as it was little more than a barn. It was called Jubilee Barn, sounding much grander than it actually was. An inspection under the Education Act of 1870 resulted in a requirement that the accommodation be enlarged to provide room for eighty children, both girls and boys. A school board was formed in 1873, but although a new premises was opened, the accommodation was still less than satisfactory, because by 1891 there were 102 children on the roll. The Board of Education warned that the buildings were insufficient, and with the help of funding from Gamlingay School board, a new school was built and ready for occupation in 1897.

Everton School, 1926. Photo: Unknown

Although it was taken a year before Tom moved to the village, the pupils in the school photograph would have been known to the family and probably some of them would have been friends with the children.

By 1927, the school had become a council junior mixed school for children up to the age of eleven. This meant that the older children must have gone elsewhere, and the attendance dropped to around fifty or so. In the mid 1930s, it was down to thirty seven, less than half the number for which the school was designed. Today, the school caters for children between the ages of three and nine and has between forty and fifty pupils on the roll.

Everton Lower School - Present Day. Photo: © Ben Harris[139]

The school, now known as Everton Lower School still stands at the original location opposite Tom's house in Potton Road. The roof of the old building is visible behind the front and side extensions.

What Tom did for work while living in Everton will have to remain a buried secret, but as he didn't drive and Everton is in a rural area he most likely returned to his old skills of agricultural labouring on one of the nearby farms.

The Later Years

Dudley Street

Tom was fifty two when he and Violet moved to 4 Dudley Street in 1936. Eldest daughter Joy was in London and would have been twenty one, just one year away from being married. Betty was seventeen, Peter thirteen, John twelve and David, the youngest, would have been ten when they left Everton for a new life.

4 Dudley Street, Bedford. Photo: © Hollands Smith[140]

The houses in Dudley Street south of Castle Road were built around 1900[141], so number four was relatively new when the family moved in. The size of the house looks deceptively small viewed from the front, but it has four bedrooms, and the downstairs rooms run back a long way from the street. The kitchen, scullery and store rooms were all accessible from inside the house. The scullery had a granite work surface by the window, where Violet would chop large blocks of salt into granules. At the back of the kitchen was a meat safe, which was just a wooden cupboard with a metal gauze front, and maybe that's where most of the salt went.

Tom and Violet at Dudley Street, c1950. Photo: Courtesy of Carol Cannell

Past the kitchen, the outhouse provided a storage area for coal and kindling, and last of all was a toilet. Outside, Tom found room to grow flowers along the edge of the narrow yard at the side of the house, and some small trees at the far end.

 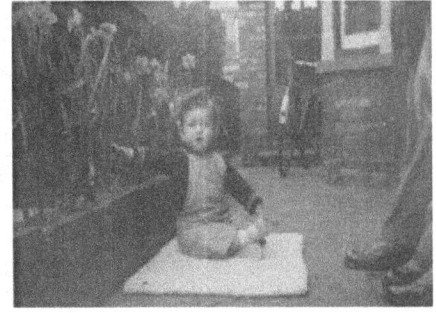

4 Dudley Street Back Yard, Pat the Spaniel (left), Author (right) c1950. Photos: Author

Although still recognisable as the old house, the property has been modernised and some of the internal walls removed. The outhouse rooms and toilet have been merged into a large kitchen/dining area, and the wall between the front room and living room has been removed.

4 Dudley Street Present Day. Photo: ©Hollands Smith[142]

Laxton's Nursery

Tom's first job after moving to Bedford was as a labourer at Laxton's nursery. The main entrance was on Goldington Road between Polhill Avenue and Pearmain Close. The nursery, which opened in 1903, was well-known for breeding new varieties of fruit and vegetables, and one of these was Pearmain.

Entrance to Laxton's, Goldington Road. Photo: Unknown

The grounds of about 140 acres stretched the length of Polhill Avenue almost to Kimbolton Road, and across to Poplar Avenue with a width to about halfway up what is now Haylands Way.

The nursery also had a shop at 63a High Street, Bedford, a stone's throw from The Rose where Tom worked as a groom in 1903. The Laxtons traded through both world wars, going into voluntary liquidation in July 1957. WW2 brought tragedy to the family when Ted Laxton (1894-1942), a partner in the nursery, was killed in a direct hit on his home at 176 Kimbolton Road during an air raid.

On the 15th February 1936, shortly after Tom joined, Edward Laxton wrote a letter to The War Office in Whitehall asking for confirmation that he was entitled to use the rank of captain. The letter intimated that Tom did not appear to be the sort of person to have held such a rank. The War Office refused to confirm, and Edward Laxton wrote again on the 28th February 1936 and in un-couched terms shared his suspicion that Tom was an impostor and using a rank to which he was not entitled. The War Office again declined to give confirmation, but revealed that they had a Captain T. Wadner on record 'who might be identical with the subject'.

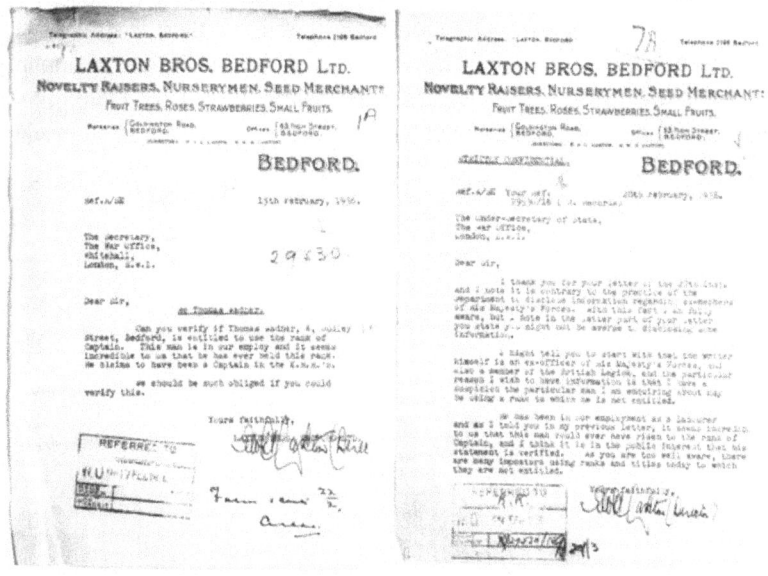

Letters from Laxton's to War Office 1936. © National Archives (OGL)

What instigated the request can only be a matter for conjecture. It could be that Tom stated on his application for employment that he was a captain in the KRRC and Laxton's became suspicious, perhaps considering that labouring would be above the station of a captain in the British Army. It could be that Tom reacted badly to something he was asked to do and pulled rank. Edward Laxton was himself an ex-officer of HM Forces, so it could be there was a power struggle between the two of them. We shall never know.

The Castle Press

Perhaps unsurprisingly, the job at Laxton's was not to last long, and by 1939 Tom was working as a packer at Robins Giblin Porter Printers in Newnham Street, Bedford. The owner changed over the years, but the print works was always known locally as Castle Press.

On the 23rd March 1939, Tom signed his son John to an apprenticeship as a Machine Minder. John was fifteen at the time, and the apprenticeship was to last six and a half years. The Second World War interrupted his training, and John served in the RAF between 1942 and 1947. On his return, he continued the apprenticeship but under the new company W.P. Griffiths. He completed his training in October 1948. It is interesting that all of the indenture witnesses lived in the same area not far from the printing works: Bower Street, Dudley Street and Denmark Street. Commuting was clearly not required back in the day.

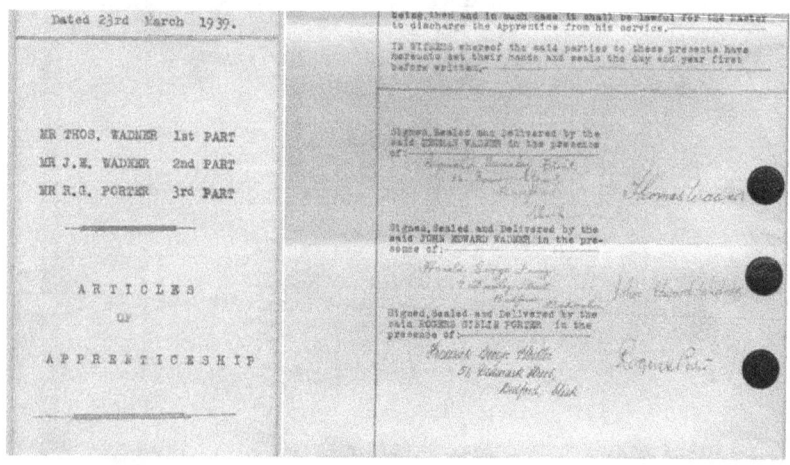

Indentures for John Wadner's Apprenticeship at Castle Press. Photo: Author

Printing at that time was very different from now, with manual typesetting. Compositors would select individual metal letters from rows of boxes and place them in the correct order, before transferring rows of type to large frames. This was known as page setting, with one frame for each printed page. Images were etched onto metal plates, and these would be fixed to wooden blocks before being placed as required between the type. Small expandable blocks were used to adjust the position of the layout and keep everything tightly in place within the bed. The printing machine would roll an inked cylinder over the bed, and press paper against it to transfer the inked image. This method, known as letterpress printing, largely gave way to offset printing in the second half of the century where the image is first transferred photographically to a thin metal plate placed on a revolving cylinder, and inked rollers transfer it to the paper. This made the process quicker and more economical, and is still in use today.

The introduction of computers and new digital printing techniques to the printing industry required less investment in operator skills such as compositing and reading, but much more in terms of capital expenditure. The Castle Press closed down in the early 1970s.

The Castle Press, 1951, one year after Tom left. Photo: ©Historic England[143]

1939 was going to be the last period of normality for five years, as the country balanced on the brink of WW2. Daughter Joy had married two years earlier and was living in Cumbria. At 4 Dudley Street, daughter Betty was working at Biddenham Dairies as a book-keeper, Peter was working as an electrician's mate at Bedford Battery in Wellington Street, John was busy at his printing apprenticeship and David, thirteen, was still at school.

Tom was too old to be called up to help with the war effort. Given his military background, and his involvement with the Everton Branch of the British Legion, he might have been tempted to volunteer for the Bedford Home Guard. However, there is no record of his participation, and perhaps that is not surprising as he had made a huge contribution during WW1. He continued to work at The Castle Press, latterly as a caretaker, until he retired in 1950.

Retirement

A short ride on his bicycle from Dudley Street to Russell Avenue, along the edge of Russell Park, a right turn into George Street for a few yards then left along Kingsley Road, brought Tom out on Newnham Avenue. A turn to the left and about one hundred yards to the right he would have swung into a large field of allotments.

Tom had two adjacent plots, located about halfway between Newnham Avenue and Barkers Lane. Each allotment was about twenty five feet wide and about one hundred feet long, about ten poles in area. Tom's twenty poles stood to the north of what was the central track from Newnham Avenue at the time, although now the allotments to the south have been given over to a large playing field.

Allotments, Newnham Avenue, Tom's ringed. Photo: Google Maps

Not all of the allotments had the luxury of a shed, but Tom had erected one for his tools, and with just enough room for a wooden kitchen chair in case it started raining and he had to shelter for a while. An old metal cistern collected enough rain water to keep the plants alive. He might well have eaten sandwiches as he took a break from digging and gazed at the Goldington Power Station, in full view across the fields from Barkers Lane. Its magnificent chimneys and cooling towers would belch steam as the generators provided 180 megawatts of electrical power to Bedford and the surrounding areas until it was decommissioned in 1983 and demolished in 1987[144].

Goldington Power Station. Photo: Mervyn Askew[145]

Tom would regularly fill the basket on the front of his bicycle with potatoes, onions, beans, peas, carrots, Brussels sprouts and salad vegetables as well as horseradish roots for home-made horseradish sauce and bunches of chrysanthemums, carnations and other beautiful flowers. His son John took over one of the allotments in the early 1960s when Tom and Violet moved from Dudley Street to the Lovell Memorial Cottages in Oakley in 1963.

Lovell Memorial Cottages

The Lovell Memorial Cottages at Oakley were built in memory of Sidney Howard Lovell with money from his father's will. Sidney was William George Lovell's only child and died aged just thirteen[146]. The will instructed that the houses 'be semi-detached and substantially built of red brick with small front gardens containing rose trees and small back gardens containing fruit trees'. The beneficiaries of the houses were to be over sixty years old and retired agricultural labourers from a list of Bedfordshire villages which included Ravensden, Thurleigh, Renhold and Goldington.

Tom met all of the Trust's requirements, and he and Violet moved in to number 26 Lovell Memorial Cottages in 1963.

Entrance to Lovell Memorial Cottages. Photo: Google Streetview

26 Lovell Memorial Cottages. Photo: Google Maps

Access to the cottage complex is by one of two entrances, and all the cottages can be reached by road. The front gardens are laid to grass with no fences or hedges, although there is a small area close to the cottages which can be planted with flowers or small bushes.

Tom and Violet outside their new cottage at Oakley, 1963. Photo: Courtesy of Ian Rushforth

The back gardens have no fences either, which makes them appear more spacious than they actually are. They are about one hundred feet in length leading down to a grassed area with a large tree at the bottom. Some of the tenants have dug the area furthest from their cottage to grow vegetables. A few yards further on, a hedge indicates the boundary of the cottages and over that are open fields. The view from the rear of the cottages is unbroken countryside. Tom cultivated a large vegetable patch which provided a year-round crop of seasonal vegetables, and tended his beloved walnut tree. This produced enough each year for Violet to fill a few jars of delicious pickled walnuts.

Although there are a variety of styles on the site, number 26 is a single floor bungalow. The side door opened into a utility room, and from there into the kitchen. The living room was large enough to accommodate a dining table for eight, needed for visitors at Sunday lunch. Strangely, the door to the hall was placed across one corner of the room. It led to the two bedrooms and to the front porch. Beyond the porch was the rarely-opened front door. In the 1960s, it was not considered good manners to enter someone's house through the front door, unless you were clergy or perhaps an officer of the law.

Tom would sit in the corner of the living room opposite the hall door, between built-in cupboards and a window which looked out to the back garden. There were no other easy chairs in the room, so visitors would pull out one of the dining chairs. A sideboard ran along the wall between the kitchen and the hall doors, adorned with a few photographs and an overly ornamental brass clock showing a neoclassical figure. Regrettably the clock no longer works. It is gilt bronze, stands thirteen inches tall, and was manufactured in France around 1820, just after the death of Napoleon.

Tom and Violet's French 'Empire' Clock. Photo: Author

Violet suffered a massive heart attack and died on the 4th October 1966 aged seventy six, when she was on holiday at her daughter Joy's house in Meopham. After a service at St. Mary's Church, Oakley on the 8th October 1966, she was cremated at the Bedford Crematorium in Fosterhill Road. Her ashes were strewn in the Garden of Remembrance.

Tom died aged eighty six on the 28th May 1971 at the Renny Lodge Hospital, Newport Pagnell. He had been suffering from osteoporosis and prostate cancer, but died from bronchopneumonia after fracturing his right humerus and a number of ribs. He was cremated at the Bedford Crematorium in Fosterhill Road on the 5th June, 1971. Like Violet's, his ashes were strewn in the Garden of Remembrance.

There is a certain injustice that someone who fought on the Western Front and survived two World Wars, should be taken by falling down a step.

Descendants

Tom and Violet's children, taken in 1985. Photo: Unknown

It didn't need much of an excuse for the siblings to gather together, and often this would be at a time of celebration such as their children's weddings. This is a rare photograph just of them.

From the left seated is Betty, John and Joy and from the left standing is David and Peter. Sadly they have all passed on. Joy was the first in 1994 and most recently Peter in 2010. Each one of them left behind strong memories, and the following vignettes offer a very brief glimpse into their lives.

Freda Joy (1915-1994)

Joy, as she was known to all, was born on the 4th March 1915 in a small cottage behind the Baptist Chapel in Chapel Yard, Ravensden. She was not to meet her father until he was repatriated on the 15th January 1919 when she was almost four years old.

The only one of the siblings who might have remembered living at 119 Gladstone Street and the farm cottage at South Pillinge, Joy would have been five years old when her father took over the license at The Polhill Arms in Renhold in 1920. By the time the family left for Everton in 1927, she would have been almost a teenager and the eldest of the two sisters and three brothers.

When the family moved to Dudley Street in 1936, Joy had already been living in London for a few years working as a lady's maid providing personal and trusted help to a stage professional. She married in Islington in July 1937, and the couple took a large apartment in London N7. Shortly after giving birth to her first child while staying with her in-laws in Reading, Joy moved to Silloth on the Cumbrian coast. With the outbreak of the Second World War she returned to Bedfordshire, and spent the war years in Fosterhill Road close to Bedford Park. It was there that her second child was born.

After the war, Joy moved to rural Kent where by 1952 two more children had arrived. She lived there until her death at the age of seventy nine on the 25th May 1994.

Betty Winifred (1919-2001)

Betty was born in Gladstone Street, Bedford on the 26th November 1919. As a babe in arms, she moved to South Pillinge Farm near Marston Moretaine and then at just under one year old to The Polhill Arms in Renhold. In 1927 she left with the family for Everton, where she attended Sandy Church School, then on to Dudley Street where she stayed until 1947. During the war years, Betty was book-keeper and worked behind the counter at Biddenham Dairies on Bromham Road, Bedford.

Charles Frossell, son of Arthur Frossell whose father was renowned for his fine cattle breeding, caught Betty's eye at the dairy. Charles and his two brothers took over the running of Wick End Farm after their father died in an accident driving a horse and cart in April 1947, and in June that year Betty and Charles married. In 1949, they moved from their house in Lansdowne Road to live at the 350 acre farm.

The dairy herd took a great deal of overseeing with milking twice each day, haymaking through the summer months, and in later years there were sheep and pigs to look after. In the early days the 17th century farmhouse had few modern conveniences. Water was pumped into the kitchen sink from a well, and cooking was carried out on a cast iron range. However, there was one new development - a telephone, Oakley 293.

After thirty years at Wick End Farm, the family moved to Bromham where, in October 2006, Betty died aged eighty six.

Arthur Peter (1923-2010)

Peter was born at The Polhill Arms, Renhold on the 10th January 1923. He was a keen sportsman, and at the age of sixteen played football for Bedford Athletic AFC.

After leaving school, Peter joined Bedford Battery in Wellington Street, Bedford as a lad delivering items locally on a bicycle, before becoming an electrician's mate and then storekeeper. Two years later in 1941, he joined the RAF for the duration of the Second World War. He was stationed at RAF Greenwood in Nova Scotia, Canada which was mainly used for training aircrew, and it was there that he qualified in the trade of electrician. Peter was posted to RAF Glatton, near Peterborough, in 1944 from where the USAAF flew B-17 Flying Fortresses on heavy bombing missions over Germany.

The war did not dull Peter's enthusiasm for football, and he played for the Glatton Services team in 1945/46, Bedford Avenue 'A' team in 1947/48, and then the newly formed Bedford Argylls.

Bedford Battery kept Peter's job open while he was away during the war, and it didn't take many years for him to work his way up to foreman. He could recall from memory the part number of anything in stock, and knew precisely where it would be found. With twenty years of trade knowledge behind him, he started up his own motor factors, Peter Wadner Ltd, on the 7th June 1966.

Peter died on the 5th September 2010 at the age of eighty seven.

John Edward (1924-2004)

John was born at the Polhill Arms in Renhold on the 23rd September 1924. During his childhood and teenage years living in and around the Bedford area, he excelled at athletics and sports. The Second World War saw him joining the RAF as an aircraft technician posted to North Africa, where he suffered a serious accident which left him with leg injuries that put a stop to his athletics ambitions.

After the war John spent most of his working life in the printing trade, starting off his career at the Castle Press in Bedford. He was offered a management position at A J Frost in Rugby around 1953, where he stayed for many years before moving back to Bedford as a senior manager at EJ Days in Clapham Road. Deciding on a career change, John became head caretaker at Mark Rutherford School in Wentworth Drive in the early 1980s, but soon found his way back into printing at Anglia Graphics in Bedford, from where he retired in 1989.

Following a heart bypass and valve replacement operation in 1994, and beating throat cancer in 1999, John suffered a serious stroke in 2002 that badly affected his speech and mobility. After a second stroke a year later, and a long stay in hospital, he had a fall and it was from this that he never recovered and died on the 9th April 2004.

After John's funeral, there was a small get-together at The Polhill Arms of his brother Peter, son and daughter-in-law Philip and Christine, and nephews and nieces Jean, Carol, Michael, Peter and Sandra. The group gathered in the exact place John was born some seventy nine years earlier.

David Thomas (1926-1998)

The youngest of the siblings, David was born on the 16th August 1926, a year before the family left The Polhill Arms in Renhold to move to Everton. He spent his early years growing up in a rural environment until moving to Dudley Street in 1936.

When the Second World War broke out, David was thirteen years old and still at school. He just caught the end of the war, and although his brothers Peter and John had joined the Royal Air Force, David enlisted in the Royal Navy. He served until August 1947, and then joined the Merchant Navy where he continued his life at sea on the SS Vin River until he was discharged in July 1948.

A fully trained engineer, David started work at the Igranic in Bedford as a machinist when he left the Merchant Navy. After marrying in 1950, he moved to Mile Road in Bedford. Like most engineers, the first thing he did was to build a huge well-equipped workshop at the bottom of the garden. David would spend much of his spare time tinkering with mechanical and electrical engineering projects and repairing broken items. The workshop survives to this day.

David stayed with the Igranic and its successor companies for the rest of his working life, some 43 years, and retired from his final position as a foundry grinder in 1991. Never motivated to move, he lived at the same address until he died in 1998 aged seventy two.

References

[1] Agar, N. (1981) The Bedfordshire Farm Workers in the Nineteenth Century

[2] http://faculty.econ.ucdavis.edu/faculty/gclark/papers/farm_wages_&_living_standards.pdf

[3] https://www.measuringworth.com/calculators/ukcompare/relativevalue.php?use%5B%5D=CPI&use%5B%5D=NOMINALEARN&year_early=1670&pound71=&shilling71=&pence71=2&amount=0.008333333333333333&year_source=1670&year_result=2018

[4] http://forebears.co.uk/surnames/smith

[5] http://forebears.io/surnames/wadner

[6] https://www.ancestry.co.uk/name-origin?surname=Wadner

[7] https://en.wikipedia.org/wiki/English_language_in_southern_England

[8] https://familysearch.org/wiki/en/Illegitimacy_in_England

[9] https://en.wikipedia.org/wiki/Knobstick_wedding

[10] https://www.ancestry.co.uk/mediaui-viewer/tree/3015612/person/6958756138/media/4f9bd946-20d4-404b-a279-90725b8d0d83

[11] http://www.genuki.org.uk/big/eng/BDF/EatonSocon/ListedGaz1868N

[12] http://www.genuki.org.uk/big/eng/BDF/LittleStaughton

[13] http://bedsarchives.bedford.gov.uk/CommunityArchives/Little-Staughton/Education-in-Little-Staughton-Before-1900.aspx

[14] http://bedsarchives.bedford.gov.uk/CommunityArchives/Little-Staughton/Education-in-Little-Staughton-Before-1900.aspx

[15] http://maps.nls.uk/geo/explore/sidebyside.cfm#zoom=17&lat=52.2394&lon=-0.3747&layers=168&right=BingHyb

[16] http://www.visitoruk.com/Bedford/little-staughton-C592-V24944.html

[17] https://en.wikipedia.org/wiki/William_Calcraft

[18] http://bedsarchives.bedford.gov.uk/CommunityArchives/Little-Staughton/The-Last-Days-of-William-Bull.aspx

[19] http://bedsarchives.bedford.gov.uk/CommunityArchives/Little-Staughton/Victorian-Murder-in-Little-Staughton.aspx

[20] https://genealogy.stackexchange.com/questions/2526/did-son-in-law-have-a-different-meaning-in-mid-19th-century-england

[21] http://projectbritain.com/year/november.htm

[22] https://www.timeanddate.com/holidays/uk/guy-fawkes-day

[23] https://greatstaughton.com/

[24] http://maps.nls.uk/view/101567744

[25] The Bedfordshire Farm Worker in the Nineteenth Century pp 11, 31

[26] http://maps.nls.uk/view/101567744

[27] Bedfordshire Times and Independent Saturday 13th June, 1896

[28] https://www.tracesofwar.com/sights/76062/Commonwealth-War-Graves-St-Mary-Churchyard.htm

[29] http://www.stevengibbs.me.uk/RavensdenMarriages.htm

[30] https://www.ancestry.co.uk/family-tree/tree/51733085/photo/24?pgn=32911&usePUBJs=true&_phsrc=BSg2235

[31] Bedfordshire Mercury November 14th 1902

[32] Bedfordshire Times and Independent February 5th 1904

[33] Bedfordshire Mercury June 20th 1902

[34] Bedfordshire Times and Independent April 22nd 1921

[35] https://www.facebook.com/Bedsatpeace/photos/a.446345885554162/446345898887494/?type=3&theater

[36] http://bedsarchives.bedford.gov.uk/CommunityArchives/Bolnhurst/Bolnhurst-School.aspx

[37] http://bedsarchives.bedford.gov.uk/CommunityArchives/Bolnhurst/Bolnhurst-School.aspx

[38] http://search.findmypast.co.uk/record/browse?id=gbor%2fschool%2fbed%2fsdthurleigh_1_1%2f0235

[39] https://en.wikipedia.org/wiki/1889%E2%80%9390_flu_pandemic

[40] http://histclo.com/schun/country/eng/chron/19/19l/dec/esc1890.html

[41] Bedfordshire Mercury March 11th 1898

[42] Lincoln Rutland and Stamford Mercury May 11th 1883

[43] https://www.anglianwater.co.uk/_assets/media/history-of-grafham-water.pdf

[44] http://bedsarchives.bedford.gov.uk/CommunityArchives/Bedford/TheRosePublicHouseBedford.aspx

[45] http://ampthillbrewhouse.co.uk/about-us/history-of-ampthill-brewing/

[46] http://www.edwardianpromenade.com/servants-2/outdoor-servants-the-stables/

[47] http://www.bbc.co.uk/education/guides/zmgxsbk/revision/7

[48] Daily Express, Children at War, July 13th, 2017

[49] http://childrenofthefuture.leeds.ac.uk/2015/06/29/how-were-british-children-affected-by-the-second-boer-war/

[50] https://en.wikipedia.org/wiki/British_Empire

[51] https://www.tommy1418.com/wwi-facts--figures--myths.html

[52] http://1914-1918.invisionzone.com/forums/topic/257847-is-this-a-krrc-uniform-please/

[53] http://rgjmuseum.co.uk/our-story/peninsula-barracks/

[54] https://www.heritage-explorer.co.uk/web/he/searchdetail.aspx?id=9770

[55] http://maltaramc.com/regsurg/rs1900_1909/rmo1904.html

[56] http://maltaramc.com/regmltgar/60th.html

[57] http://maltaramc.com/regmltgar/60th.html

[58] https://britishinterventionincrete.wordpress.com/tag/british-army-crete-1905/

[59] https://en.wikipedia.org/wiki/Anglo-Egyptian_War

[60] http://www.krrcassociation.com/index.php/history/11-battalion-locations-1755-1965

[61] Hampshire Telegraph 7th October 1910

[62] http://riflesmuseum.co.uk/?tag=krrc

[63] http://www.britishbattles.com/firstww/battle-mons.htm

[64] http://www.britishbattles.com/battle-of-the-aisne/

[65] https://commons.wikimedia.org/wiki/File:The_First_Battle_of_the_Aisne,_September_1914_Q51499.jpg

[66] http://www.historyofwar.org/articles/wars_race_to_sea.html

[67] https://mitchamwarmemorial.wordpress.com/2014/10/30/private-j-j-twyman-2nd-bn-royal-sussex-30th-october-1914/

[68] http://1914-1918.invisionzone.com/forums/index.php?%2Ftopic%2F134364-1st-battalion-krrc%2F

[69] The National Archives reference WO339/13716/RC1244771

[70] The National Archives reference WO339/13716/RC1244771

[71] http://1914-1918.invisionzone.com/forums/index.php?/topic/134364-1st-battalion-krrc/

[72] https://en.wikipedia.org/wiki/World_War_I_prisoners_of_war_in_Germany

[73] https://www.abebooks.com/CREFELD-German-P.O.W-Camp-Great-Photograph/19015785528/bd

[74] http://1914-1918.invisionzone.com/forums/index.php?/topic/82249-crefeld-pow-camp/

[75] http://scholarworks.wmich.edu/wwi_pow_camps/890/

[76] The National Archives reference WO339/13716/RC1244771

[77] http://www.h-net.org/reviews/showrev.php?id=24137

[78] https://en.wikipedia.org/wiki/Holzminden_prisoner-of-war_camp

[79] Durnford, H.G. 1920 The Tunnellers of Holzminden, Cambridge University Press

[80] http://www.wereldoorlog1418.nl/refugees/vluchtelingen/militairen.html

[81] https://search.findmypast.com/bna/viewarticle?id=bl%2f0001464%2f19190115%2f118&noTouch=true

[82] http://www.simplonpc.co.uk/PO_Liners2.html#Khyber1914

[83] The National Archives reference WO339/13716/RC1244771

[84] The National Archives reference WO339/13716/RC1244771

[85] http://www.mkheritage.co.uk/nbhg/docs/1891map.html

[86] Bedfordshire Mercury August 17th 1900

[87] Bedfordshire Archives Reference Z1479/2/5 1937

[88] Bedfordshire Times December 26th 1919

[89] http://virtual-library.culturalservices.net/webingres/bedfordshire/vlib/0.digitised_resources/leighton_digitisation_timeline.htm

[90] http://www.norwayheritage.com/p_ship.asp?sh=ionia

[91] http://www.doukhobor.org/Ship-Descriptions.html

[92] http://www.wrecksite.eu/wreck.aspx?13082

[93] https://en.wikipedia.org/wiki/Regent_Park

[94] https://www1.toronto.ca/wps/portal/contentonly?vgnextoid=c3db757ae6b31410VgnVCM10000071d60f89RCRD&vgnextchannel=7cb4ba2ae8b1e310VgnVCM10000071d60f89RCRD

[95] https://www.ncbi.nlm.nih.gov/pmc/articles/PMC1488685/?page=2

[96] https://www.jstor.org/stable/41972736?seq=1#page_scan_tab_contents

[97] http://wolvertonpast.blogspot.co.uk/2011/11/co-op.html

[98] The National Archives reference WO95/1371/2

[99] The National Archives reference WO95/1371/2

[100] Sheffield Telegraph 21st November 1914

[101] https://www.gutenberg.org/files/51387/51387-h/51387-h.htm

[102] https://archive.org/stream/cu31924030726735/cu31924030726735_djvu.txt

[103] The National Archives reference WO339/13714/RC1336118

[104] http://search.findmypast.co.uk/record?id=TNA%2FR39%2F5011%2F5011E%2F004%2F14

[105] http://old-southampton.tumblr.com/

[106] Devon and Exeter Gazette 24th November 1906

[107] Southern Daily Echo 25th February 1907

[108] Hampshire Advertiser 22nd September 1906

[109] https://www.flickr.com/photos/lselibrary/24606518058/

[110] https://www.derbyshire.gov.uk/leisure/record-office/derbyshire-record-office.aspx

[111] http://checkmypostcode.uk/mk442rb#.WVpHsITyvJU

[112] http://www.ravensdenvillage.org.uk/Jan2011/History/whoswho65.htm

[113] Bedfordshire Archives reference WW1/AC/OP2/63

[114] http://bedsarchives.bedford.gov.uk/CommunityArchives/Bedford/HigginsAndSonsBreweryBedford.aspx

[115] https://www.europeanbeerguide.net/beer1917.htm

[116] http://publin.ie/2015/the-price-of-a-pint-from-1928-2015-in-todays-money/

[117] Bedfordshire Archives reference DV1/C6

[118] The National Archives reference WO339/13716/RC1244771

[119] http://www.genuki.org.uk/big/eng/BDF/Misc/BDF/BedfordshireSchoolsRecords

[120] Kelly's Directory of Bedfordshire 1885, p.103

[121] https://books.google.co.uk/books?id=NnFbAAAAQAAJ&pg=PA8&lpg=PA8&dq=boys+and+girls+school+renhold&source=bl&ots=KKa6o_psHI&sig=2Xox-Idu4-0-Gao9pbjSVJfshKI&hl=en&sa=X&ved=0ahUKEwi_vZyYt6nUAhWjAcAKHZ9NAOI4ChDoAQgpMAE#v=onepage&q=boys%20and%20girls%20school%20renhold&f=false

[122] Bedfordshire Mercury 8th February 1862

[123] Bedfordshire Mercury 4th March 1904

[124] Bedfordshire Times 31st August 1869

[125] Bedfordshire Times 18th September 1925

[126] Bedfordshire Times and Independent 31st August 1923

[127] http://www.evertonvillagehall.org.uk/evertonsoldiers.html

[128] http://bedsarchives.bedford.gov.uk/CommunityArchives/Everton/The-Parish-of-Everton-in-General.aspx

[129] https://upload.wikimedia.org/wikipedia/commons/c/c1/Gray1824.hunts.jpg

[130] Biggleswade Chronicle and Bedfordshire Gazette 21st March 1930

[131] Biggleswade Chronicle and Bedfordshire Gazette 19th September 1930

[132] Biggleswade Chronicle 16th November, 1934

[133] http://www.roll-of-honour.com/Bedfordshire/EvertonRollofHonour.html

[134] http://www.geograph.org.uk/photo/2019126

[135] Biggleswade Chronicle 27th February 1931

[136] Bedfordshire Times 2nd August 1935

[137] Bedfordshire Times 21st December 1934

[138] Biggleswade Chronicle 9th August 1935

[139] http://www.geograph.org.uk/photo/2769875

[140] http://www.zoopla.co.uk/property-history/4-dudley-street/bedford/mk40-3tb/40822136

[141] http://www.mouseprice.com/property-information/ref-15288155

[142] http://www.zoopla.co.uk/property-history/4-dudley-street/bedford/mk40-3tb/40822136

[143] https://britainfromabove.org.uk/en/image/EAW037751

[144] http://discovery.nationalarchives.gov.uk/details/r/faae65e1-b6d4-4a1f-b6bb-40a4da50f58b

[145] http://www.bedfordrivervalleypark.org.uk/heritage/goldington/

[146] http://bedsarchives.bedford.gov.uk/CommunityArchives/Oakley/LovellAlmshousesOakley.aspx

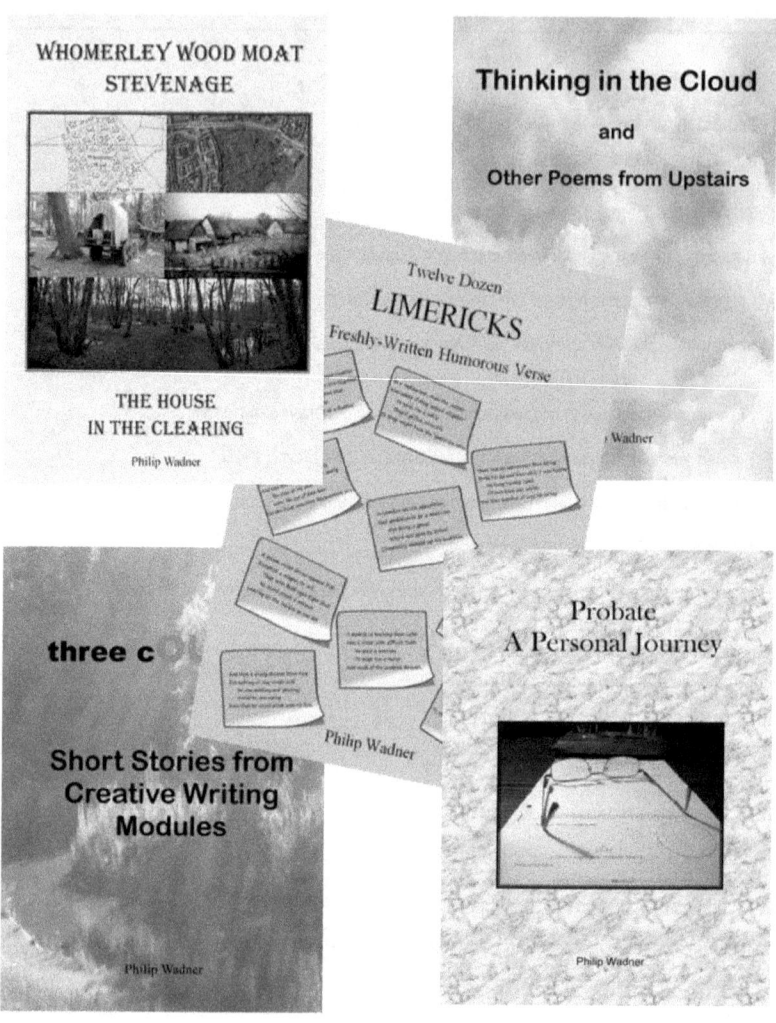

These books by the same author are available to order from good booksellers, or online from Amazon (including Kindle) or Lulu.

Visit www.cadebooks.co.uk for more ways to purchase, including signed copies.

www.ingramcontent.com/pod-product-compliance
Lightning Source LLC
Chambersburg PA
CBHW061649040426
42446CB00010B/1661